Dedicated Lives

Dedicated Lives

STORIES OF PIONEERS
OF WOMEN'S FOOTBALL
IN AUSTRALIA

GREG DOWNES

First published in 2021 by Fair Play Publishing
PO Box 4101, Balgowlah Heights, NSW 2093, Australia

www.fairplaypublishing.com.au

ISBN: 978-1-925914-04-7
ISBN: 978-1-925914-05-4 (ePub)

© Greg Downes 2021
The moral rights of the author have been asserted.

All rights reserved. Except as permitted under the *Australian Copyright Act 1968* (for example, a fair dealing for the purposes of study, research, criticism or review), no part of this book may be reproduced, stored in a retrieval system, communicated or transmitted in any form or by any means without prior written permission from the Publisher.

Cover design and typesetting by Kiryl Lysenka.

Back cover: Nell Parry
Thanks to all who dipped into their personal photo collections for most of the images in this book.

Other photos: Dr Roy Hay, Football Far North Coast, Getty Images.

All inquiries should be made to the Publisher via sales@fairplaypublishing.com.au

 A catalogue record for this book is available from the National Library of Australia

Contents

Introduction		1
1.	Elaine Watson OAM	5
2.	Betty Hoar	15
3.	Theresa Deas	26
4.	Vicki Bugden	42
5.	Janelle (Nell) Perry	50
6.	Dalys Carmody	58
7.	Deborah Nichols	66
8.	Heather Reid AM	76
9.	Carolyn Monk	85
10.	Maggie Koumi	88
11.	Sharon Young	105
12.	Lisa Casagrande	112
13.	Belinda Wilson	117
14.	Nicky Leitch	131
15.	Paul Turner	143
16.	Louisa Bisby	153
17.	Jane Natoli	162
18.	Annette Hughes	170
Look how far we've come		178
Acknowledgements		181
About the Author		182
Note from the Publisher		183

Introduction

Women's football in Australia is riding a new high. The national team, the Matildas, is well and truly on the world stage. High participation, equal pay success, increasing resources and support, and record crowd attendances and online viewers have all contributed to greater media focus. The wider public has opened its eyes to the women's game and embraced it, lifting the Matildas to be one of Australia's favourite sporting teams.

The icing on the cake came in June 2020, when FIFA announced that Australia and New Zealand would co-host the 2023 FIFA Women's World Cup. The move provides an unprecedented opportunity for the women's game to build on this recent success and establish itself as a major player within the mainstream of Australia's sporting consciousness. The tournament will also promote gender equality in Australia by showcasing the talents of the best women footballers in the world doing what they do best: playing football. And through their skill and determination, these athletes will help dispel long-held sexism around sport—the belief that women are less capable than men.

But while it is pleasing to witness women's football in Australia come of age, the game's history hides a decades-long story of struggle and determination by pioneers whom historians have mostly ignored.

Women's football in Australia can be traced back more than a century to the early 1900s. Women were playing the game unregulated during WWI, the Great Depression and WWII. Newspaper evidence suggests that 'ladies' teams were formed in Parramatta (NSW) in 1903 and Candelo (NSW) in 1908. Games were also reported in 1916 in West Wallsend in Northern New South Wales, in the Maitland District in 1928, Speers Point in 1929 and Corrimal in 1930. A Women's Soccer Football Association was formed at a meeting in Lithgow in 1931. In Queensland, newspapers of the day also reported two clubs forming in Toowoomba, City and Rovers, in 1921. And Brisbane's first women's team, Latrobe Ladies, formed that same year.

In his book, *Chronicles of Soccer in Australia: the Foundation Years 1859 to 1949*, Peter Kunz notes that a schoolgirls' match in Toowoomba, Queensland, was reported on in 1917. The Sydney Ladies Football Association was formed in 1921, followed one month later by the formation of the Queensland Ladies Soccer Football Association. Fiona Crawford and Lee McGowan, in their book, *Never Say Die: The Hundred-Year Overnight Success of Australian Women's Football*, state that reports of women playing football are more clearly and regularly documented during this period, and the records show that the number of women's teams founded would not be surpassed until the 1960s.

The first public game of women's football is widely acknowledged as being between North and South Brisbane on September 25 in front of a crowd of 10,000 at the Brisbane Cricket Ground (the Gabba), as a curtain-raiser to a game of men's Australian rules football.

And so, women's football emerged in the early 1920s. But reports of the game soon began to fall away. What little media attention survived often denigrated and trivialised those women who continued to play. The male-dominated clubs and associations followed the example of the press, discouraging women with such open discrimination that sexism became widespread and institutionalised during the 1920s. Indeed, it was the ingrained opinion of most organisations that women should not be allowed to play football. Reports of women's football after 1926 subsequently become hard to find; however, there are records of games occurring during WWII and into the decades leading up to the 1960s. McGowan states the women's game was nearly lost during this period.

After WWII, rising immigration helped both the men's and women's game resurge. Historians often ignore the latter group's contributions, yet the influx of migrants created opportunities for the wives and girlfriends of their male partners to take up the game—and with those newcomers came one of the leading pioneers of the women's game in Australia, Pat O'Connor.

O'Connor emigrated from England in 1963 and was instrumental in forming the Bass Hill women's team in 1965, where her husband was playing at the time, and she went on to form the Metropolitan Ladies Soccer Association (MLSA) in 1967. Pat played as captain of Sydney Prague and St George Ladies teams for 10 years. But although women's teams were becoming more plentiful during the 1960s, it wasn't until the 1970s that the game took on a more structured form. This was a time recognised worldwide as the decade in which women's football began to take a foothold, and by 1974, regular women's competitions had been established in most states of Australia.

The first international women's game to receive official recognition was when New Zealand competed for the Trans-Tasman Trophy in a three-test series in Sydney and Brisbane in October 1979. The first game was held in Sydney, resulting in a 2–2 draw.

But unofficially, the first Australian international was in 1975, when the Australian Soccer Federation (ASF), with Sir Arthur George as president and Brian Le Fevre as secretary, endorsed the NSW squad of 15 (12 St George players, two from Ingleburn and one from Eastern Suburbs) to represent as an Australian XI team and participate at the first Women's Asian Cup in Hong Kong. The players were given permission to wear the green and gold jersey with the embroidered Coat of Arms. While the NSW team was not an official Australian side, local and international media recognised it as such at the time.

Since then, the Matildas have qualified for a total of 10 major world tournaments, including three Olympic Games, and have played more than 400 international matches, continuing to go from success to success.

As a result, the sport is now starting to receive the media attention it deserves. Although this is still in its infancy, among social media, television broadcasters, fans of the sport and wider society, there has emerged a growing call to recognise the pioneers of the game. This book is an attempt to do so.

These powerful stories represent a history of long-deserved recognition and acknowledgement of past efforts and successes that have remained untold. They reveal how the women came to play or be involved in the game, the hardships they faced and what playing football meant to those who pioneered the sport in Australia.

The writing of this book has taken me some years to get together after I completed my PhD in 2016. However, the stories of the women pioneers whom I met and interviewed as the basis for my thesis have always stayed with me, and I have never lost the desire to make them part of the history of the women's game in Australia.

I have let the women's stories take the main stage and the book has enabled them to share their experiences in their own words. It is by no means an exhaustive list, but I hope that it gives readers a greater understanding of some of those involved in building the women's game here.

There are many stories still to be told.

My hope is that this book will create an interest in seeking out these stories, to gain first-hand knowledge of the beginnings of women's football from those that experienced it, and to let that inform the history of the game.

Greg Downes
Northern Rivers, NSW
September 2021

1. Elaine Watson OAM

*I opted for soccer.
My father could never understand it.*

Elaine Watson OAM came to women's football in 1974. In that same year, Elaine, as an executive member of the Brisbane Junior Soccer Association, put her hand up to manage the Queensland women's team in the first national women's championships held in Sydney. The first board of the newly appointed Australian Women's Soccer Association (AWSA) was also elected at these championships and Elaine was elected as its first vice president. That year was to mark the beginning of a lifetime devotion to the development of women's football in Australia. Elaine spent 18 years involved with the AWSA and is recognised for her work as an administrator, coach, referee and as the manager of the national women's team.

Elaine has been awarded many accolades along the way, most importantly her OAM, which she received in 1993 in recognition of her work in the development of the women's game in Australia. Elaine contributed to the written history of the game by compiling two publications: *Australian Women's Soccer: The first 20 Years*, in 1994 and *Women's Soccer in Queensland: In a League of Its Own*, in 1997. She is truly a 'matriarch of women's football'.

After a promising start in the early 1920s, women's football in Queensland began to fall away. The press only intermittently reported women playing the game into the 1930s, and those who continued to play throughout the WWII years and into the 1950s had to constantly rally against uninterested, male-dominated clubs and an unsupportive and negative media. It wasn't until the late 1960s that signs of the game began to re-emerge and competitions would take hold. According to historians Crawford and McGowan, the Brisbane women's football competition was the first to form in Australia in the early 1960s, with seven teams competing weekly.

It was during this time that the Watson family became involved in football.

Elaine Watson was born in Brisbane, the eldest daughter of five children. She came to football in 1963 thanks to her two sons and youngest daughter taking up the game and her husband Arthur being elected to the executive of the Brisbane Junior Soccer Association (BJSA).

I first met Elaine Watson OAM on a sunny spring morning at her home in Brisbane on September 3, 2012. I had travelled to Statesmen Crescent, Sunnybank Hills—named after the General Motors Holden Acacia Ridge factory nearby—to interview her as part of my PhD thesis. I fondly recall Elaine answering the door and proclaiming, after I introduced myself, that she had an OAM after her name and could I kindly refer to her using the full title. I was a little taken aback at first, but after spending some time with her came to realise how important the recognition implied by the Order of Australia medal was to her. She was awarded it in 1993 for her work in the development of women's football in Australia. However, if it wasn't for the desire of her two boys and youngest daughter to play football, Elaine may have been lost to the game. You see, the Watsons were originally a hockey family. As Elaine explained:

> I was actually a hockey person and so was my husband. He was an Australian hockey umpire and when our eldest son got to be six years old we said, 'Well, son, do you want to play a sport, do you want to play hockey?' And he looked at me and he said, 'Oh no, Mum, those sticks they could hurt you.' (Laughing.)
>
> The kids over the road played soccer and it was the same rules, the same positions, only they kicked a bigger ball and there were no sticks, so that's how come we got involved in soccer.

While Elaine was convinced that the change from hockey to soccer was a good family choice, her father was not so easily swayed. Elaine's grandfather, George Watson, had been involved in the break away from rugby union and the formation of the Queensland rugby football league in 1908.

> I come from a family where my grandfather was involved with rugby union, and he was the first assistant secretary of rugby league when they broke away from rugby union. So there I've got rugby union, rugby league, and then I opted for soccer. My father could never understand it. (Laughter.) I said, 'Well, your father changed, and I've changed too.' I was a hockey girl and changed to soccer. Same game, different-shaped ball and no sticks!

Both Elaine and Arthur became involved in the BJSA as both of her two boys were playing. Not one to sit back and rely on others to do the work, Elaine was elected as the assistant secretary of the association in 1971. At that time, the Brisbane women's football competition, which, according to football historians McGowan and Crawford, had likely formed prior to 1961, was still under the guardianship of the BJSA. According to Elaine, the women realised they must form their own association when it became clear that the BJSA would have to split into a northern and southern division due to the increasing number of registrations.

Since the smaller number of women players would not support two competitions, Elaine acted. She convened a meeting in her home with Arthur and a group of other supporters, including Bob Geoghegan (coach and manager of the Annerley ladies team) and Keith Barclay (coach of the Coalstars). Together, they established a sub-committee that eventually led to the election of the first executive of the South Queensland Women's Soccer Association (SQWSA) in 1976. All four would be life members.

By 1974, regular women's competitions had been established in most states of Australia. According to Elaine Watson's publication, *Australian Women's Soccer: The First 20 Years*, 'for those women playing the game it was becoming increasingly important that they be recognised as serious sportswomen and that their sport was afforded credibility'. During that year, Pat O'Connor from the Metropolitan Ladies Soccer Association (MLSA) in Sydney and Dr Oscar Mate, president of the Western Australia Women's Soccer Association (WAWSA), campaigned to contact all of the associations known to conduct women's competitions. The pair wanted a commitment from them to begin a national championship, and to raise the idea of a national women's association.

And so it was in August 1974 that five states took part in the first national championships, held in the Sydney suburbs of Granville, Centennial Park and Bankstown. The teams were not true representative state teams at the time: the St George club formed the majority of the NSW team, Morley Windmills formed the basis of the WA team and a Greensborough/Melton combination played for Victoria. Macquarie and Districts represented Northern NSW, and BJSA made up Queensland.

> Apparently, the Western Australian people got together with the Sydney people, and they decided to organise the first national championships for women and they invited each of the states. New South Wales had two associations, the New South Wales one and Northern New South Wales. The Brisbane Women's juniors ran the Brisbane Women's competition and ... in later years a north Queensland Association was formed because I reckon

if NSW had two associations Brisbane deserved the same because we're a much bigger state than NSW.

At that time, Elaine was secretary of the BJSA, and their policy was to always send an executive member with a representative team. As there were only two women on the executive at that stage, Elaine put her hand up:

> Hazel Pickup said that she did not want to be concerned with women's soccer, and I put my hand up. I had six weeks to choose the team and outfit them and whatever. Mind you, when we got down there we were the only team in a uniform. We had nice denim slacks and shirts and so all the girls looked like a team.

New South Wales won the championships. Afterwards, a meeting was held—under a tin shed in the pouring rain, Elaine recalls—to establish the first national association. It would go on to guide the development of women's football in Australia.

> Well, they elected the first Australian Board at those first championships in Sydney. The thing was they hadn't notified Queensland they were having a meeting so there was no one there from Queensland. When I found out what had happened, I had a little bit of a discussion about it and they actually invited a chappie who was secretary of the BJSA, Frank Clark, to become vice president of the newly formed Australian Association. Frank said he wasn't going to have anything to do with the women's competition and put my name forward. So I became vice president of the newly formed AWSA and it just grew from there.

Oscar Mate from Western Australia was elected president and Pat O'Connor from NSW as secretary, and Elaine went on to become president of the association in 1978, a position she held for 11 years.

Back on the homefront in 1977, SQWSA had begun a search for suitable land to build a headquarters and field, which would include dressing rooms, a referee's room, equipment storage and a canteen. Eventually a venue was identified in an area now known as Atlanta Field in Geebung. Elaine played a major negotiating role in securing the land and the required funding for the necessary works. In 1980, she secured a building loan of $10,000 by acting as joint guarantor with her husband, Arthur. Both were later recognised on an honour board of Life Members, Guarantors and Donors, and a special mention was made of Elaine's work at the opening ceremony.

After the first national championships, AWSA decided that all future championships would be held annually, and each state would take it turn to host. By 1981, the national women's championships had expanded to include up to nine states and territories, and a youth championship was introduced in 1985. Elaine was involved with the organisation for 18 years, and even developed its first constitution.

Never one to take a backward step, Elaine often volunteered to take on roles that men had historically dominated. Prior to women's football, she coached the young boys' teams and went even further to become Australia's first female qualified referee. The lack of suitable referees for the women's game and the attitudes of those male referees who had a different opinion on whether women should play was not the only issue confronting the women. Those who took up the challenge and trained to be referees were themselves often confronted by widespread discrimination.

> Because we were always short of referees, they were having a referee's exam there and went around the clubs calling for volunteers and I volunteered—incurable volunteer, that's me. They sent the exam up from Brisbane and I sat and I passed, and I refereed games up there in the juniors. The next year I took a course of 12-14-year-old boys through to become cadet referees, spread the numbers because at least they could run the lines and signal offside and that sort of thing.
>
> We came back to Brisbane the following year, but they wouldn't recognise me as a referee down here because I hadn't sat for the exam here, so I had to sit again and it was the same exam. And I had the president come up to me saying, 'Elaine, Elaine, you know you've passed the exam, you're a referee!' I said, 'What did I get?' And he said, '99.5%', and I just looked at him and he said, 'What's the matter?'—'Where did I lose 0.5%?' (Laughing.)

Elaine's willingness to get involved, along with the initiative of both the Mackay and Brisbane referees associations to let women undertake refereeing qualifications, provided a platform for more women to get involved.

> You know, they started with the juniors but, particularly the women, they soon graduated to seniors because there weren't the numbers there to keep them isolated. They sort of spread their assistance; they might have played in one area and refereed in another, you know. So Queensland has, I'm told,

the largest number of qualified female referees in Australia, and some of them are even FIFA qualified.

Elaine's husband was not to be left out, of course.

> As a family we got involved. Arthur got his referee's ticket as well and, because his background is in the catering industry, he ran the canteen for us at our home ground, and his firm supported them financially so he was recognised as a benefactor of women's soccer.

Arthur was awarded life membership of SQWSA in 1985 for his contribution to the women's game in Queensland. He spent 10 years as vice president and helped develop the canteen and fields at the new headquarters in Geebung. He was also recognised for his role as MC at the many presentation nights and Player of the Year Awards. As Arthur says in Elaine's book, *Women's Soccer in Queensland: In a League of Its Own*, after Elaine got involved in the first national championships in Sydney, 'from then on it was Go, Go, Go with both of us up to our ears in women's soccer'.

From there, the movement continued growing. In 1985, AWSA granted the national champions' (NSW) approval to compete in the Asian Cup, held in Hong Kong in August. At the same meeting, AWSA agreed to affiliate with the Asian Ladies Football Confederation (ALFC). AWSA was by now administering a sport that was rapidly developing both domestically and internationally. And Elaine was again crucial to the effort. To alleviate the workload of the volunteers, she helped secure $25,000 from the Australian Sports Commission (ASC) for assistance with the appointment of a National Executive Director (NED)—a role that went to Keith Gilmour.

Elaine was also instrumental in moving the national headquarters to Canberra in 1985 to facilitate interaction with the ASC, which was beginning to take a greater interest in promoting women and girls' participation in football.

Some historical references say Elaine was 'sometimes a divisive figure' and 'not well liked by the men in the game'. This may have arisen from her dedication and drive to achieve what was best for women's football. When I asked her if she had ever faced any opposition due to being a woman, Elaine was quick to reply:

> (Laughter.) They might have liked to try it, but I'm tougher than that. I found that if you stand up for things in a quite reasonable tone, they really can't argue with you because you're speaking reasonably and they think to

themselves, 'Oh yes, if that was our sport, that's the way I'd speak too.' So I did have a great range of acceptance, I feel. I never got into any problem areas which made me feel like going and jumping in the creek or anything like that. Oh well, that's the way it goes, you know. It happens and you've just got to deal with it, and the other side of that coin is that there were so many people with nice attitudes that made you feel welcome and feel appreciated. Worth its weight in gold, really.

However, there was one regret that Elaine clearly felt strong about: her failure to secure the presidency of AWSA in 1984.

> I tell you what, it was a real blow when I lost the Australian presidency, it really was; it truly struck me because it wasn't that I'd done anything wrong, it's just that someone else wanted to be the boss and they had different ideas to me. They couldn't say that I'd made a stuff-up of the whole shebang, you know, because we were financially established and representative established and things like that, but it wasn't good enough for him and that was a real blow. I reckon if it had have been someone I admired, I could have taken it better, but because I didn't think all that much of him with his attitude and everything, it was a real blow to find that the majority of the other states had voted with him.
>
> So I came back to Brisbane. I think I might have mentioned that I knocked six strokes off my golf handicap in that year, but then Ian Brusasco co-opted me to serve on the men's association because he told the newspapers that I was the best administrator he'd ever struck. In that year I had phone calls from Victoria, South Australia, Tasmania, Western Australia—Elaine, Elaine, make sure you come back. (Laughter.) They were not happy with the things that were happening so Queensland nominated me the next year and I swept back in. So that was my one and only defeat. I have resigned from several positions, but I have only been defeated that once.

Elaine also had success on the international stage. She was appointed as the first manager of an Australian team when one comprised mainly of NSW and Western Australian players participated in the first Women's World Invitational Tournament in Taipei in 1978. However, it wasn't until the following year that an Australian team played their first officially recognised international competition in a three-way Trans-Tasman Trophy series against New Zealand. Elaine was again appointed as joint manager (alongside Noelene Stanley) for the series, which was held in September 1979.

Some years later, Elaine helped develop the Oceania Women's Football Confederation (OWFC) after being elected president of a steering committee formed to recommend a suitable structure. And she was subsequently elected as vice president of the confederation at its first meeting in October 1982.

> Then there was contact from New Zealand because they are our closest neighbour, and they had women's teams and a women's organisation and they wanted some international competition. We all got together and decided to form Oceania Women's Football because the men had the Oceania Football as an extra for them, but it was all the men's competitions. So there was an Oceania Women's Football Committee there for quite some time.

Elaine was to play a large role in the management of Australian representative teams over the coming years as the national team became more involved in international football tournaments. From 1978 to 1993, the national senior team competed in 17 international events. Elaine was involved as tour leader or team manager for tours undertaken in 1978, '79, '80, '83 and '85. The canvassing of FIFA by AWSA and other footballing nations eventually led to the development of the inaugural FIFA Women's World Cup in 1991 and the inclusion of women's football in the Olympic Games in 1996.

Elaine fondly remembers her experiences with the women who played in national championships and international events—one experience particularly.

> Oh god, well I know when the second Australian championships were held in Brisbane and the Queensland team, as they were known then, took me and dunked me in the shower after it had finished. (Laughter.) Because they were so pleased to have the event done here. (Laughter). They told me they wanted to say thank you and that's why they dunked me in the shower. (Laughter.) I mean, they're the sort of things that stay in your memory and you laugh because you've enjoyed it, you know. I think in one of those books there's a photo of me with a towel wrapped around me and a fist shaking like this as I came out of the shower. (Laughter.) There's been such a lot of interaction, which makes you feel really good, and I think that's what does it. Like having my Victorian friends still sending me Christmas cards, you know, and I think 'Oh god, yes, and Theresa Deas, she was the goalkeeper, I think she was in the first Australian team'—and so it goes back a long way.

In 1989, after 14 years in national office, 11 as president, Elaine decided not to stand for the presidency and took on the role of Director of Finance. She remained a member of AWSA for several more years and played a major role in the development of the Women's National Soccer League (WNSL), which began in 1996. Elaine resigned from AWSA duties in 1993, the year she was awarded with an OAM for her services to women's football.

However, it wasn't until 2007 that Elaine finally relinquished her role in women's football when she stepped down from Football Queensland disciplinary committee.

> I've been involved for almost a lifetime, you know. It's only five years since I've called it quits. I was on the Brisbane executive at that stage, which were men, women and juniors and all amalgamated. Life member of the Queensland Association, which also then became combined men, women and juniors. So I am the only dual life member they've had, life member of the men and life member of the women, and then they amalgamated and the CEO rang me to ask which of my life memberships I would like to surrender and I told him neither. I was going to use the second one to come back and haunt them if they didn't do the right thing. (Laughter.)

When I asked Elaine what her involvement in the game has meant to her, she reflected on how sport can play an important role in a person's life.

> Well, it's been an extra life really. Of course, you've got your own family at home and they're going through school, and they're got their club and representative involvement—our eldest boy played under-15s representative soccer. But then they grow up and they start living their own lives. They marry and leave home and so your involvement with a sporting activity is something that helps to fill the gaps. You look at any club and they've got a range of administrators from the grey hairs down to the just-out-of-high-school people because it sort of flows through when people have the time and the interest they devote to something that gives them that satisfaction. If they go to work and they've got a boss who hounds them and then they go to soccer and they coach the boys' team, it's a different story, it's a relaxation and a reward for them, so I think sport has got a big part to play in any rounded life.
>
> I think you've got to all be open to what's happening, to try your best, to try to achieve the best, that's what it's about really, and sometimes you win and sometimes you lose, and if you lose you've just got to think where did I

go wrong, let's try better, try harder and if you pick up next year—hey presto, it's all working.

Elaine has received many awards over the years in recognition of her involvement and service to the development of women's football in Australia—she is very proud of each. They include life memberships with SQWSA in 1979, AWSA in 1981 (the first ever awarded) and the Queensland Soccer Federation in 1989. Elaine received an Award of Merit from the Confederation of Sport in 1992 for outstanding service to Australian sport (the first soccer administrator to be so honoured) culminating with her OAM in 1993. Elaine is particularly proud of her inclusion in the FFA Hall of Fame in 1999, and in 2010 Brisbane Football named the Premier women's trophy as the Elaine Watson Cup to honour her services to the game.

Heather Reid, an FFA Board member, guest speaker and friend of Elaine Watson, described the OAM recipient as a 'matriarch of women's football in this country'. When I asked Elaine about it, she said,

> I'm just glad that I was available when I was available. Because I think it was my input from the beginning that was very much needed. Even though later on, you know, I realise you do better this way and do it better that way. But there always has to be someone that leads the way, and I consider that I was lucky to go in at that time and have the space and the direction to promote the code the way it was promoted. I was happy to be a part of it, and I'm not the only one that had good ideas ... Betty Hoar was one of the early ones and Theresa Jones, as she was then.
>
> I met such a wide range of lovely people that wanted to work for the good of everyone, and I think that's the best part about it.

2. Betty Hoar

I loved every minute of it!

Betty Hoar began playing football for the Luton Ladies club in London in the 1960s. She migrated to Australia with her family in 1970 and was soon to become one of the most prominent women in the development of the game. Betty brought her playing skills and the coaching experience of her husband, Mick, to Victoria where both became involved in the early days of women's football. While Elaine Watson was making her way in Queensland, Betty was asked to set up one of the foundation clubs in Victoria women's football—Greensborough Ladies, with Mick as the first coach, in 1974.

Betty helped set up the Victoria Women's Soccer Association (VWSA) and was seconded to the AWSA by Elaine Watson in 1979. Betty spent six years as the association's secretary and served with the association for 10 years. She continued to play the game until the age of 49. She has served the women's game as a player, coach, administrator and has managed a number of Victorian teams in international tournaments, including the national tour of New Zealand in 1981, the Oceania Cup in Hawaii and New Caledonia in 1985, and Brisbane in 1989.

Betty, with her husband and family, have dedicated their lives to the development of women's football in Victoria and Australia.

The 1960s saw many women's football teams form across the country, including in Victoria. But games were often irregular. Hay and Murray highlight one between the Slavia women's team and Cobram at Olympic Park on March 31, 1963— promoted with a photo of the Slavia team on the front page of *Soccer News*. Likewise, in the early 1970s Mrs Lynette McKernan had a vision of starting her own girls' soccer team. Her two sons played for the Doveton juniors and her husband was on the committee. Both her daughters, Julie and Lyn, were eager to play. Over a short time she had recruited enough girls aged 14 to 18 years to form a team.

Lynette, a founder of the Doveton Ladies, says her team played the Morwell Pegasus Ladies on July 6, 1972 for the opening of the new Doveton Soccer Club pavilion. And the Doveton Ladies also played the Frankston Pines team on July 13 that same year.

Other matches, while important, were played in the shadow of the men's games. For example, on July 1, 1973, the Victorian men's team were to play Cruzerio from Brazil at Olympic Park, Melbourne. The Victorian Soccer Federation wanted the two strongest women's teams to play a curtain-raiser, so Doveton Ladies and Bayswater were selected, with Rosa Vloedmans as referee.

It wasn't until 1970 that women in Victoria began talking about the formation of a social competition to help organise the occasional games. Historian Ted Simmons states in *History of Football in Australia* that consequently a 10-team social competition was formed that year, which included teams from Frankston, Bayswater, Doveton, Clayton, Sunshine, Ajax (St Albans), Melton, Melbourne, Werribee and Oak Park. Yet discrimination was rampant, just as it was in many male-dominated organisations and clubs in Australia. Historians Roy Hay and Bill Murray state in their book, *A History of Football in Australia: A Game of Two Halves*, that in 1960 the Victorian Amateur Soccer Football Association (VASFA) council issued a ban on girls wanting to play in boys' teams. Registrations would not be accepted until a full girls' team could be formed.

I asked Betty about her upbringing in England:

> I actually didn't know where I was born because I was adopted. My mother was Irish, and a couple adopted me when I was four and they lived on a farm. This was down in a place called Wittersham in Kent (England). I actually found out when I had my confirmation. They had to know where I was born, and I said, 'Well, I was in this home, so I don't know where I was born.' But the adoption was in London and anyway I found out: 'Oh, you were adopted'—'Oh, was I?' Which meant absolutely nothing to me, and when I told my adopted mother she almost flipped and said, 'You shouldn't have known!'

Betty's interest in soccer began during those early years on the farm.

> I started when living on the farm and my old dad would take me around and throw a tennis ball at me. We'd often take the dogs for a walk. I didn't have a soccer ball then, but as I said, we lived in a little village, and I'd go up there on the Saturday mornings before they played the game and I'd kick the ball with them and do whatever. That's how long I've been involved. It's been a passion of mine, well, I suppose from since I was born.

England in the mid-1940s was beginning to wake up from the many hardships and tragedies it faced during WWII.

> Funnily enough, we didn't have television in those days, but the English soccer game used to be on a Monday night and my mum would say, 'Come on, Liza, time for bed.' And I'd sit outside the kitchen door listening to the game and all of a sudden, I'd hear, 'Are you up those stairs yet?' (Laughter.)

And then on February 6, 1958, a European British Airways flight crashed just after taking off from Munich airport, killing 23 passengers. Among those who died were eight players from the Manchester United Soccer Club—it was to be a lasting memory for Betty.

> It happened on my birthday in 1958; I was 16. Oh, oh, I cried for days.

At 17, Betty was encouraged to leave the farm and travel to London for work. While living in Luton she met Mick and by 19 was married and playing soccer. This was in the late 1960s.

> We went to a function one particular night because we all sort of met each other at social clubs and whatever, and one of the girls said, 'We want to start a women's soccer team,' and Mick says, 'No, you don't!' (Laughter.) I said, 'Oh, great.' And it was called Luton Ladies. He was the coach and we had great fun.

News of women playing soccer in England soon hit the press in Australia, and women there began reading about the escapades of others playing football.

> We actually made the Herald Sun over here when I was pregnant with my first child, Tracey. I was expecting her, and we went up to Tottenham, a team in London, and somebody called our goalkeeper a rather rude name—and this is in the back of the Herald Sun in 1966 or '67. My friend from here, who'd come over here, sent it to us and I thought, 'Oh god,' and it said the coach's wife Betty is crying her eyes out because of all this sort of thing. (Laughter.)

Betty and Mick migrated to Australia just when women's football was finding its feet. She had just given birth to their second child, Jason (who would play a major role in the development of the women's game in Victoria). And the couple soon began their long careers in football in Australia.

> In 1972, Mick took up soccer with a club, and in 1974 I had a phone call and they said, 'Betty, we believe you played soccer in England, would you be happy to help start another team?' I said, 'Oh, great,' so this was the Greensborough Ladies. So we started this team, and Mick was the first coach. The first year we only had four teams: Greensborough Ladies, Green Gulley, Melton and Doveton.

Simmons argues that the more serious women were dissatisfied with the social competition developed in 1970 and wanted a proper women's association to control the game. Until this point, women had the complete support of the men's clubs in their areas and could use the men's grounds and facilities. But the dominance of the men's associations and the AFL-focused media hindered the push to form a more professional women's association. Simmons writes, 'After three years of talks, Melbourne women finally took the bold step of organising a meeting with a view to officially creating a state women's association. They called a secret meeting at the Siemens building in Richmond in 1973 which approved the formation of the Victorian Women's Soccer Association (VWSA) with Fred Habbe as the first president and Jacqui Ager, goalkeeper for the Frankston Pines women's club, as secretary.'

Ager was to go on to play a major role in the administration of the game in Victoria and as a member of the executive of the AWSA. She was elected as treasurer at the inaugural meeting of the organisation in 1974. According to Betty, Ager 'was more important than me because she actually started the women's league in Victoria'. Representatives of 14 women's teams attended the meeting, and two weeks later announced they wanted regular access to clubhouses, soccer fields and general coaching assistance. In all, more than 200 women agreed to form the new association and organise a women's soccer league—it was the start of something big.

So the VWSA was formed alongside the inaugural state women's competition, which was initially split into a western and eastern division. This structure continued until the competition collapsed in 1984. McGowan and Crawford, in their book *Never Say Die: The Hundred Year Overnight Success of Australian Women's Football*, state that the circumstances of the collapse are poorly known, but women were evidently playing football at that time. A state competition did not re-emerge until 1992 when the Victorian Women's Premier League was instituted.

Meanwhile, women's football was growing rapidly in the other states, and Oscar Mate (WA) and Pat O'Connor (NSW) campaigned to contact every association that ran women's competitions to establish a national championship and develop a national association. Five organisations agreed to enter an inaugural national championship held in Sydney in August 1974. A combination of players drawn from the Greensborough, Melton, Doveton and Green Gully clubs represented Victoria. Betty recounts her involvement:

> And towards August, they were going to have their first national championships, Queensland, New South Wales, Victoria and Western Australia, and we had our first tournament in Sydney near where the railway crash was, Granville, and the four of us went. Ray Langdale was coach, Fred Habbe, who was a big sports guy, was the first president of the VSWA, and they had by this time invited me onto the committee and said would I go as manager? So I did. I got the job as manager for Victoria.

Some last-minute withdrawals found Betty taking a more direct role than she had anticipated.

> Anyway, we went up to play and one particular game—there weren't any hard-and-fast set rules—we went there and three of the girls didn't turn up. Well, we only had two subs, and somebody said, 'Well, you'd better play,' so I actually partook in that first game.

Victoria's first attempt at securing the national crown went poorly. As the least experienced of the states competing, Victoria came away with three losses, the worst being to NSW six goals to one, and a draw. Betty summed it up best. 'We lost, we came last.' Victoria had to wait until 1987 to win its first national title at the championships held in Alice Springs.

Back off the field, Betty was to hold several positions with the state association, including registrar, and was elected as secretary in 1984. While registrar, Betty and fellow trailblazer Maria Berry fought the VASFA over its sanction against women and girls playing soccer, which had been in place since 1960. In 1985, Betty was elected vice president and the VWSA executive was increased to include Betty's son Jason Hoar as competition officer. By the late 1990s, the VWSA had grown to such a point that the voluntary nature of the organisation could no longer support the increase in player and competition numbers.

After a stint as Public Relations Officer for the VWSA, Jason went on to become president in 1991 and continued in that role until 1997.

> He was actually very good because Jason is good with words and organisation and what. In fact, at committee meetings, he used to tell me to shut up.

> (Laughter.) Jason actually became the commissioner of the Victorian Soccer Association (VSF) for the women's soccer. So he then became more important than me. I was just one on the committee.

By 1998, Jason had moved to the Board of the VSF where he was to play a major role in the negotiations surrounding the amalgamation of the VWSA with the state men's body.

At the annual general meeting (AGM) of AWSA held after the sixth national championships in Darwin in 1979, long-standing state representatives Pat O'Connor (NSW) and Oscar Mate (WA) both decided not to run for board positions due to heavy work commitments. The chair of the AWSA, Elaine Watson, was quick to secure a prominent Victorian representative.

> Well, Elaine Watson came up to me and said, 'Betty, would you be interested in being secretary of the AWSA?' I said, 'I'm not very clever with words; I have to write everything down and tape everything.' I said, 'Okay,' so that was 1979.

Betty held the position until 1985.

At the AGM held late in the same year, Betty took on the role of AWSA Director of National Teams and Tours, a position that suited her down to the ground. She had previously undertaken the duties of AWSA team manager for the 1981 New Zealand provincial tour—the first tour to have an all-female contingent of officials, including tour leader Irene Sneyd, coach Trixie Tagg (the first female coach of an Australian women's team) and Annet McKenzie from South Australia as the physiotherapist. In 1983, Betty was selected as the team manager for the Wahine Tournament in Hawaii, which included three test matches. Australia won all three and consequently the Aloha Trophy. In November and December of the same year, Betty managed the team at the first Oceania Cup played in Noumea, New Caledonia, alongside teams from New Zealand, New Caledonia and Fiji. She later managed the first Australian international youth team to travel overseas at the Dallas Cup Youth International in the USA in 1986. Australia reached the semi-finals of the competition, which was dominated by the strong USA club teams.

1989 brought fresh successes for the Hoars. Mick (Betty's husband) was made assistant coach for both the Australian Green and Gold teams, which were competing in the third Oceania Cup tournament in Brisbane. Betty was elected team manager of the Gold team. That year Betty was also elected Director of Coaches and Referees for the AWSA—perhaps for her life-long involvement in the development of women in coaching and refereeing in Victoria.

> I actually start my coaching career with my young son when he was six or seven. He wanted to play soccer, so we went down to the old Greensborough High School. There were 24 little boys there and one of them was starting to cry. I said, 'What's wrong?' And he said, 'We haven't got a ball.' We got a ball and I played 12 against 12. But nobody wanted to go in goal, and one little kid said, 'I'll play, Mrs Betty, I'll play.' I said, 'Okay.' He had a shirt on and it fitted him up to here at the start of the game, and then we had rain, and rain, and rain. By the end of the day, the shirt was down to his ankles, and he said, 'Did we win, Mrs Betty?'—'No,' I said, 'we only let 12 in, but don't worry.' (Laughter.) I can still remember that day. I coached them for a year and then actually my son Gavin took over.

Betty was also involved with coaching her daughter's football team at school.

> When my daughter went to Grimshaw Primary, her and another girl said, 'We don't want to play any sport, can we play soccer?' I said, 'Yeah, course you can.' The teacher said, 'I know nothing about soccer except that the ball is round. I'm taking the footy team. Will you take the soccer team?' I said, 'Yeah, okay.' I had a great time.

But when she became Director of Coaches and Referees for the AWSA, Betty faced bigger challenges than a lack of footballs.

While slowly being accepted as players and administrators, women still faced strong male opposition as coaches and referees. To make a place for women, Betty (and other Victorians such as Jane Natoli, Nicky Leitch and Debbie Nichols) saw it as essential that they get involved. Indeed, one of the biggest hurdles for women playing football was securing suitably qualified referees. Women's football was not seen as important and was largely unrecognised by the male-dominated authorities. This had a lasting impression on how the women I interviewed experienced and remembered the game.

> One of my biggest problems, and I will say this, is referees. One said to me one day, 'Well, we don't class you as important.' I said, 'We're playing the same sport as those boys, and we want referees.' And when we had finals, he said, 'Oh well, we'll send so and so.' I said, 'Is he qualified?'—'Well, no, he's only 16 or 17.' That was one of our biggest problems, accepting us as senior girls. Senior boys get a referee, and we did have lots of hassles there. As I said, my biggest problem in my day was the referee situation, which is, I think, why I took it up.

And it was during her time as a referee that Betty felt that she received the most opposition to her involvement from the male-dominated institutions that ran the game.

> I'll tell you, there was an amateur group of soccer players, an amateur organisation. They reckoned that we were only good enough to be amateur association referees. I said, 'We all pass the same tests. I took the same tests as Chris Bambridge who is one of our best referees. He was a FIFA referee and we had to take all those tests the same, so we have to be treated the same.' And it took girls a long while to be accepted as refs. Especially when you went on a Saturday or Sunday morning and you had to do a local game—I always used to ref in Lalor or Thomastown, and these guys would say, 'You stupid woman, go back to the kitchen.' Which they did quite often.

This opposition sometimes manifested itself in experiences of personal abuse and ridicule.

> But then you used to cop abuse when you were at interschool things. That's the only time I ever copped abuse. 'What's she doing reffing?' I said, 'Well, I'm here to do a game. Any more abuse, and I'll stop the game.' So I did, and they said, 'We're going to get into trouble, aren't we?' Well, the referees are always right and whether you like me, him or whoever. That's when the kids got a bit lippy. Tell the ref off once, you know and abuse them once, you put in a bad report about the club and the club gets fined so, I think they all woke up.
>
> Oh, you've got your stupid comments, like I was referring a game down in Dandenong and the game was pretty even and a corner was given so I blew for the corner. By the time they fannied and faffed around organising it, I blew the whistle for time out and this coach said, 'You've got to allow the corner to be taken'. I said, 'No I haven't'—'Yes you have'. I said, 'The only time you carry on the game is if there's an infringement and the time's up and the penalty is taken.' Oh, he's given me a hard time over the years. I won't mention names. He comes from Heidelberg. (Laughter.)

The lack of financial support was another major hurdle for the women to face if they wanted to continue to play the game, and it was an issue common to most.

> We didn't have a lot of help. We had to do all our own fundraising, and believe you me, the chocolate drives we've done and all that sort of thing. The only

person that ever helped, and God bless his soul, was George Wallace. I went down there one day, and he said, 'Betty, what's wrong?' I said, 'George, we're going to Sydney'—and this was 1981—'and we can't afford tracksuits.' He phoned up Teddy Whitton at Adidas. 'Ted, I want 20 tracksuits for the Victorian girls' soccer team.' That's the only thing we ever got free from the VSF. We had to fundraise. It's cost Mick and I a fortune to send me overseas. I think I had to pay for all my trips. Even my first two Australian tours I had to pay for.

Betty remarked that all the women really wanted was equal rights. As a result, Betty and the committee got involved in the fight to secure separate change rooms for the girls and women. This was a common prejudice faced by all women playing football.

We wanted to be treated exactly the same as the men and not just be put down, equal rights, yeah. As I said to Jack Riley, I met him when we had this equal opportunity thing with the girls starting, and of course that's when the thing about changing rooms came up. And they said, 'The girls have to change outside,' and I said, 'No they won't.' We used to change in the park down at Richmond, East Richmond. We used to have to change in the toilets when we had a school game. The boys changed in a room and the girls come dressed, come ready for the game. That took a long while to get sorted out, but we did eventually.

Betty and others initiated the fight to gain adequate facilities for women in football in the 1980s, but it still continues today, with government and football organisations struggling to finance the huge gap identified some 40 years earlier.

Despite the adversity, Betty retained fond memories for the game, much like Elaine Watson. 'I loved every minute of it!' said Betty. She remembers times spent with the players as manager of the Victorian state team, especially.

On this particular day, we had one Victorian girl, Melinda Martin her name was, and it always seemed that when there was a Victorian girl (I should have realised long before) there was going to be trouble because I was the Victorian manager. Anyway, we went to training and had a really good session and we were due to play a game the next day, and somebody said, 'Oh shit, what's up on the flagpole?'—'They're my bloody shorts, how did they get up there?' (Laughter.)

However, Mick was quick to point out that there was even better to come on the tour to New Caledonia for the third Oceania Cup tournament in 1983. Remembering, Betty jumped back in:

> The best one happened when we went to Noumea. Jimmy Selby was the coach; now to me, he was a very good coach. We took a team to Noumea and Hawaii. We were playing in some particular tournament, and Elaine was the manager. She was the tour leader, and she was very good at her job. Joan Monteith was the physio, very, very good. They both came from Queensland; well, that doesn't matter.
>
> I was the manageress and we had one Victorian girl, Theresa Deas, who's also in the Hall of Fame with me now, bitch! (Laughter.) The things she did to me on that tour.
>
> Anyway, we had a night out, and we were staying at the same place as New Zealand, and officially you're not supposed to talk to them and socialise and whatever. Anyway, we're at the hotel and they said, 'We're going to have a night with the New Zealand girls, and you're all to get up to do something, you know, an act, or whatever.' Anyway, we're getting ready to have this night and I'm packing the case up. I said, 'Where's all my drawers gone?' Fortunately, I'd bought all new gear. I came in and spoke to Elaine and she immediately turned her back and said, 'Oh, you just reminded me, I've got to go and do something.' This is as clear as a bell.
>
> Anyway, we had this function this night and Peewee and one of the girls from Queensland did arm wrestling with headphones on—that was funny. Two or three other stints, and then Theresa is up there announcing, 'We now have the Elisabeth Hoar underwear, what did they call it, show.' I'm sitting on the chair, and I thought, my god. I'm dreading to think that someone comes out in my green pants, panty girdle and bra. I said, 'I'll kill you, I'll kill you.' (Laughter.)
>
> Anyway, the pièce de résistance at this particular tournament was Karen Menzies from Northern NSW. When we first got there, one lot of us got there on the beach and Karen Menzies just had her bikini bottoms on, and I said, 'Karen, Elaine is coming up soon, put a bra on.' Please remember that Elaine, well, is a little bit prudish, you could say.
>
> Well, the next thing Karen comes out and she reminded me the other day, Sam Newman was on The Footy Show with a Mac and brown trilby hat, and I can't stand him anyway, and Karen comes out dressed like that. She does a

couple of twirls and she then opens the jacket and she's got my white knickers on with the Union Jack and two Union Jacks over here—well, Elaine Watson, we had to save her from falling into the bloody swimming pool. (Laughter.) They were always playing pranks on me wherever I'd gone ... (Lots of laughter.) Oh no, they were a great bunch of girls, and we had some great fun.

Betty eventually stopped playing at the age of 49. 'Because I said, "Mum's going to have an 'eart attack so she's got to stop playing soccer." So I stopped playing then. And I didn't become involved much more.'

Betty has received several awards in recognition of her role in the development of women's football; however, she didn't place a lot of importance on them until she was awarded a life membership with Football Federation Australia (FFA). Mick proudly shared Betty's award night.

> That night there, honest, I was so proud of her. I really was, you know, and normally I'd laugh at things, but we were all betting as to when she'd break down and cry because she's a very tearful person. There's all the clubs, there's the men's teams. It's the gold medal night. All the men's teams and all the women's teams and lots and lots of people there, 300–400 people, I don't know.
>
> Came her turn to get up on stage, right, she got up on stage and she walks to it and she's, she's like this, and she starts talking. And I thought, she's going to go, she's going to cry, she's going to cry and I'm going to have dash out and give her a big handkerchief and wipe her tears. And she just stopped, and she just leant on the rostrum, and then she gave it to them. She just reeled, and there was, you could hear a pin drop, everybody listened to every word she said. You could hear a pin drop and she actually spoke sense, she did, she said good stuff, she really did, and they applauded her because it really was. If you've known Betty for as long and all those kids—most of the girls that were there have known Betty since they were knee-high to a grasshopper. They stood up and applauded. It was great, it was fantastic!

Betty was inducted into the FFA Hall of Fame in 2003 and was one of only two inaugural inductees into the FFV Hall of Fame in 2010, alongside Jimmy Rooney. Betty also received an Australian Government Sports Medal in 2000 and achieved life membership with both the VWSA and AWSA in 1984.

3. Theresa Deas

I started as a right forward and I loved it, absolutely loved it, running up and down the wing and trying to score goals, it was terrific.

The development of women's football in Victoria and Australia owes much to the presence of Theresa Deas. Having migrated to Australia with her family in 1973, Theresa began playing at the age of 12 and did not hand in her gloves until she was 38 years of age. During this time Theresa represented her state as goalkeeper for 18 years, attending 12 national championships, and in 1980 was selected to protect the goal square for the national team for a further 10 years.

After retiring Theresa was involved with the VWSA from 1992 to 1999 and later worked with VSF until 2000 as the Development and Project Officer for female participation. It was during this time that major changes were occurring in the women's game. 1999, the year after Theresa left the game, saw considerable organisational changes. Theresa witnessed first-hand the impact of the amalgamation of Football Victoria (FV) and the Victorian Women's Soccer Association (VWSA) and is passionate about the work that the many pioneers had done to form the women's association. This was a tumultuous period in the game with many opposing the move.

Since leaving the game Theresa has been involved with FV and is currently a valued member of the FV Women's Standing Committee. Theresa is involved in the support of women and girls' player development, coaching and the formation of Women's National Premier League (WNPL) clubs in Victoria.

Simmons states that by 1975 the interest in women's soccer had grown so much that the Victorian state competition doubled in size, with two divisions comprising 11 teams. In the West Division were Greensborough, Melton, Green Gully, Werribee, Broadmeadows and Dinamo, while the East Division had Doveton, Repco Clayton, Dandenong, Bayswater and Frankston Pines. And it was onto this rapidly expanding scene that Theresa Deas burst when she joined Dandenong City Soccer Club. She would go on to spend over 20 years a goalkeeper, representing both Victoria and Australia, before taking on roles in coaching, administration and mentoring. Currently president of the National Premier League Club Women's Southern United and chair of Football Federation Victoria (FFV) Women's Standing Committee, Theresa remains a strong voice in women's football.

Theresa was born in Newport, South Wales in 1963 and migrated to Australia with her family in 1973.

> We came to Australia when I was 10, with my family, Mum and Dad, my brother and myself, for work reasons. Mum and Dad came searching for a better lifestyle, and we settled in Dandenong. On the way over, we came half by plane and half by boat from Singapore. It was the worst two weeks of my life on board that ship. We arrived in Perth and, while we were there, people suggested that Melbourne was the place to come and Dandenong was a very industrial town and that my parents would get work straight away. That is where we settled.

A keen player himself, Theresa's father quickly got the family involved with a football club in Dandenong. Football clubs for newly arrived immigrants often gave the families a sense of community.

> Very soon, my father—who had a great love of sport, and of course with two young children—decided that they wanted to become part of a football club. He had played for Newport in South Wales, which I think were a second division club or something at that point in time. When we came over here, we went to Dandenong City Football Club, which was very local for us, and he didn't play but he started to coach my brother's team. That was basically as soon as we arrived.

Theresa's involvement with women's football began that year, since she was constantly around the game with her brother and father. However, it wasn't until two years later, when she was 12, that she began playing.

> Of course, I got dragged to training with my brother, as Mum was out working, and even though I was older than my brother I just joined in. It ended up, most of the time, I was just kicking around with the boys and I would go in goals—there was no formal thing at all. So that was when I was about 10. I also got involved heavily with other sports at school at that point in time. I

think my brother and I were just kids who loved sport, and with Dad's encouragement that is what happened.

At the club I got to know a couple of people. It was a very English/Scottish background club, so we had a lot of friends, and someone noticed that I was doing okay with the football with the boys and said they were forming a women's team. My dad just said, 'You might as well play—you are training with the boys, you might as well play,' which is what happened, and I started off with the Dandenong City Soccer Club women's team at the ripe old age of 12.

That was the start of my career. I started as a right forward and I loved it, absolutely loved it, running up and down the wing and trying to score goals, it was terrific. During that time, I was also playing netball and basketball with other club teams. One day the goalkeeper got injured and I was just thrown in goals because I had played netball and knew how to catch the ball, and that is how I started.

So Theresa joined a group of other women and girls in the team's first season. In 1975, Dandenong joined another 10 teams to form the second year of the new women's competition. As a 12-year-old, game results were unimportant, and it was all about having fun and being part of a team. Many of the pioneer women in this book share that pleasure of simply playing the game and the physicality of being involved. As Theresa explained,

I started at 12 and, the first season, none of the girls had really played soccer before, and the ages ranged from me being 12—I think we had a married woman in the team who was in her 40s. The age range was huge, but it didn't matter because we all just were there because we had fun, we loved it. The best thing was rolling in the mud and enjoying ourselves. It was just carefree and whatever happened, happened. I remember one game we played against Greensborough, and it was 13-nil; they beat us. And I was in goals, and I remember coming off the field after the game and not having a care in the world that 13 goals had gone in and the opposition team was coming up to me and patting me on the back and saying how wonderfully I played. I thought, okay, that's all right. But it was the pure enjoyment of just being in the team that made me continue on.

The enjoyment that Theresa and so many other women in the early 1970s got from playing football was despite the only piecemeal acceptance from the male-dominated clubs. The women who played tended to stick together at the clubs in which they started because friendships developed and there existed a level of security that enabled them to develop their skills and confidence. The women placed more importance on having fun and making friends, where winning was not the most important thing.

> The core of the girls at Dandenong City pretty much stayed together. We were there for a quite a while until, I think it still happens today, when the focus is on the males playing football and not the females you just get a secondary, 'Oh yeah, the girls play!'

While the women were barely tolerated on the field, the men were happy to see them at the club as they often worked in the many behind-the-scenes roles, including working in the canteen, washing playing strips and fundraising. While these activities were necessary for the successful running of any football club, they and the women who performed the bulk of the work were often undervalued.

> We became better at what we were doing and we started to realise, a bit like women's rights in a way, that we had value and as women we were doing an awful lot of work around the club. When it first started off, most of these women playing were daughters, wives or girlfriends of the men in the club. That is how we got a team together. Those people were also the canteen ladies and the strip washers and all of those so-called female roles at the club.

Times were changing, however, and the women began to question the lack of support and resources from the clubs they were supposed to be part of. They were sick of the being treated as second-class citizens, particularly when they were starting to win games and competitions.

> As we became better, and we were actually winning a lot more games and then winning leagues, I think there was a bit of an uprising, and we decided we wanted to demand more out of this. And unfortunately, at that particular club, they weren't prepared to give us what we were asking. What we were asking was no more than what they were doing for even the junior boys: somewhere we could change in, where people weren't wandering in and out, and that we had a place that we could actually have some privacy and that the pitch would be marked and we wouldn't have to be us there hours before the game, and we weren't playing on the back field all the time.

When the club refused, many women left.

> We decided that we would go to a club that might help us a little bit more, and as it was, it wasn't far away. It was Dandenong North. They were a much smaller club that were focused on building, and we stayed there a number of years until changes in committees and more egotistical males came in, and we weren't looked after as well as what we thought we should be looked after.

That women and girls had to fight for every piece of support from the clubs during the early years of the state women's competition was common. But they remained loyal to each other.

> When things happened at Dandenong North that weren't working, I went from Dandenong North for one year to Waverley. That was because there were so many state players at Waverley that I had such good fun with. Like anything, you tend to go where your friends are going, and I wanted to go and do something different and play with the friends that I had, that we were on tour with, so I went there for a year and had a really good season. I then realised that my true heart was with my old club, and the girls that I had known for years, so I went back. That team then moved to Berwick City and then from Berwick City moved to Cranbourne Casey, which is now Casey Comets, and Casey Comets is still in the Women's Premier League.

The Women's National League was initiated in 1974 with Victoria as one of the formation states. Sydney hosted the first championship, with Elaine Watson attending for Queensland and Betty Hoar for Victoria. Theresa didn't become aware of the state championships until she was asked to attend selection trials.

> I was 14 when I was first looked at, or asked to go to the trials for state. The competition had increased very quickly. There wasn't just four teams, there was a league happening by that time. He came up to me after the game and said, 'We got a state team, why don't you come down and trial for the state team?' My dad and mother were like, 'Yeah, go for it, you love it, so have a go.' I went down and got selected in the team. The first goalkeeper was a girl called Monica Werner, who was then a current national player and for that first season I sat on the bench at the national championships and I admired her, and just wanted to be in her position.

Theresa didn't have to wait long. She made her state debut the following year at the 1978 national championships held in Newcastle.

> The next year when I was 15, Monica wasn't there, and I was in goals. That was pretty much my first national championship. I think it was in Newcastle and I went away with the team. I was the youngest and one of a lot of older girls, and I was billeted or stayed in a hotel with two older women so they could look after me and help me. My parents travelled up there to watch.

Theresa played for 18 years in the Victorian state team and attended 12 national championships (1978–1989), receiving an AWSA Gold Achievement Award in 1990 in recognition of her lengthy career.

In 1980, at just 17 and after playing for just two years as a state representative, Theresa was selected to play for the national team. The team were to play in the return Trans-Tasman Cup, held in New Zealand, following the inaugural three-test series in Sydney and Brisbane in the previous year.

> It was very early on in my career. At 17, my first tour was to New Zealand with, I can't remember who the second goalkeeper was, but the people I went away with were from all around Australia. There was everyone basically from Queensland, New South Wales and Victoria generally, and a girl from Perth, Sandra Brentnall. My memories from that time were just wonderful. We were all a very similar age range from 17 through to 25, and on that tour I was with Shona Bass, a fellow Victorian, and Andrea Martin, also a Victorian.

These tours forged many great and lifelong friendships, and Theresa is mindful of how important the early pioneers were to the game's development. 'We wouldn't be having this conversation if it wasn't for those who pioneered the game,' she reminds me.

> Even though those two players played for Greensborough, which was the big opposition team for the local competition, they pretty much looked after me—took care of me and showed me the ropes. My memories of that first tour were wonderful, because then I got to meet some great players from New South Wales and Queensland. Those people I remember as really strong pioneers of the game, and they were the ones who pushed the limits and really put women's soccer on the map, so to speak. Even though in this day

and age people don't recognise the work that those people actually did—to bring the game so it can be played today—and they are not remembered like they should be, as far as I am concerned.

In 1983, Theresa travelled to New Caledonia for the inaugural Oceania Cup and later in the same year to Hawaii to compete in the Aloha Cup, which Australia won. In 1984, she represented Australia at the Xian international tournament in China and followed this with tours to New Zealand (second Oceania Cup) in 1986, the fourth World Invitational Tournament in Taiwan in 1987 and at the pilot World Cup held in China in 1988. On these tours, Theresa often joined some of the most influential figures in the game, including administrators and managers Elaine Watson, Betty Hoar and Heather Reid. And she played alongside some of Australia's most inspirational talent: Julie Dolan, Renaye Iserief, Joanne Millman, Sue Monteath, Jane Oakley and Julie Murray.

By the conclusion of her career, Theresa had represented Victoria for a total of 18 years from 1978–1998. She played in 12 national championships, winning two in 1987 (Alice Springs) and 1989 (Canberra) and wore the green and gold for Australia 18 times over a 10-year period from 1980–1988.

> I finished my soccer career at 38 years old, my last national championship at 38 as a senior goalkeeper in Davenport, Tasmania. I had my two daughters with me and my mother, who always travelled with the children because I took them everywhere.

After her international career, Theresa remained involved in the game. She was Director for Women's Soccer Victoria from 1992–94 and Development Officer from 1994–99. In 1993, Theresa was selected as manager of the Australian Youth National Team for the Dana Cup, an annual event held in Denmark. Elaine Watson praised her ability to maintain morale, which resulted in a successful tour for the squad. From 1999–2000, Theresa took on the role as the Development and Project Officer for female participation for VSF.

> At this point obviously I married my husband. If it wasn't for the fact that I married somebody who was so supportive of my career, I would not have been able to do the things that I have done.
>
> My family got wholly involved with the whole process because my brother was playing soccer as well. Mum and Dad were both the secretaries of clubs

or president or on committees, so much so that my mum ended up secretary of the Women's Soccer Association prior to the amalgamation of the FFV. My father was the state coach. My brother has been a team manager, he has been on the Board. So my whole family was completely and utterly involved in the whole growth of women's soccer in Victoria in the very early years.

Theresa found support from those she knew in the community to help her address one of the major barriers that women faced when trying to play football in the developing years—the lack of financial support. When compared with the level of support and player wages received by the men this difference resulted in the marginalisation of the women's game by making it difficult for them to participate and succeed.

This was compounded by the general lack of understanding by the wider community and the administrators of the game about what hardship this difference created for the women.

It was hard to get sponsorship because it was only people that really knew me that helped me. For example, my mother's work sponsored me $500 because they knew about what my mother's daughter was doing. I worked for the National Bank, they knew about my career, the National Bank was really supportive in my early years. I worked for Safeway as a checkout chick, and the people who knew or had interest in their staff and had the knowledge were really supportive.

To go and knock on someone's door and say 'Hi, I'm Theresa, I'm in the national team or in a state team could you sponsor me some money, so I can go overseas?' It was really difficult. Really, really difficult, so I had to rely an awful lot on the local community that was around me to be able to help me and support me and work my bottom off to pay for everything, along with my parents, obviously, initially. I couldn't ask them to pay for everything all the time. It wasn't in me to do that, so at one point I was working three jobs.

While I was working for National Australia Bank in those early years, I still worked part time at Safeway, so I would do my full day of work and then Thursday, Friday or whatever nights I could fit in around training, I would work at Safeway to get the extra money to help me go on tour. That period from 17 through to 25, those years when I was in the national team was really hard work, both soccer and with working so I could afford to do these trips.

The lack of financial support impacted those unfortunate enough to sustain an injury. The women often had no recourse, as there were no contractual arrangements that may have offered compensation for women players.

> I was touring overseas in Hawaii with the national team. Prior to that, I had been overseas for two weeks on another tour, which is unusual to have two lots in my final year at school, and just prior to the exams I sustained a dislocated kneecap and I sat my BCE exams with my leg in a cast on a seat. There was no compensation for anybody doing any sport, particularly a girl doing a male sport at that particular point in time. It was so disappointing, and I failed just, and when the results came in, in January the next year, I was so disheartened. I didn't know what to do with myself. So I picked myself up and decided, while I was doing well in one area of my life, I better do something with myself for the future.

Theresa went back to school the following year, passed her exams and went to university for a short time to study Environmental Science.

Although she had the support of her family and friends, Theresa often faced negative reactions to her participation in the sport on top of her financial difficulties.

> Not everyone was supportive. We are talking a long time ago now, and football in my era was always looked at as a male sport—as it still is to an extent today. It is far more widely accepted today.

Theresa found that being a good player helped her navigate the many barriers that impacted women during the formative years of women's football. Gaining acceptance as footballers from male peers and the wider football community was important to these pioneering women. Yet unfortunately, their legitimacy depended on proof of ability, and they were often denied unconditional acceptance.

> Then, I think if I hadn't been a good player, it might have been different. But the proof was in me playing. At school, for example, when I came over here, I was in Grade Five, and I came over here with a very strong Welsh accent, and didn't play football, but loved sport. So at lunch time, I would be out there kicking the ball around with the boys, not soccer, football or footy, but I was a bit of a centre of attention because of the Welsh accent, so I was quite accepted by the boys and the girls. The girls wanted to listen to me, and the

boys liked the fact that I could kick the football just as far as they could. I never felt any problem with it at school.

High school posed different problems, but Theresa's footballing ability again defused some potential issues.

When I went to high school and I was playing football, I went to a mixed girls and boys secondary college, Catholic, that was run by the nuns and the brothers. When I was 14/15, I was playing for a state team; the reaction from the nuns was, 'Why are you doing that?' It didn't take very long for them to actually realise that Theresa's not doing too badly at this particular sport, if she is going away and playing for the state. By the time I was 17 and was selected for the national team, it was just common knowledge.

Being a good friend of Paul Wade (former Socceroo and Australian captain) was also helpful.

I remember playing for the school soccer team, and I was the younger girl, and I was in the company of Paul Wade—he went to my school. Paul and I were good friends; my brother and his younger brother were good friends. Paul was wonderful because he knew me. The rest of the boys in the team were very accepting, and because I was a good goalkeeper and there was nobody else at the school that was any good, it was fine. The kids were good.

But when we had to travel to other schools and we were playing against predominantly boys' schools, I can remember one of the brothers, Brother Joe—funny how these things stick in your memory—pulled me into his office and said, 'I don't think you can play, Theresa, this game we are going to St Bede's. I don't think you can play because there is nowhere for you to change, and I don't think it is right that a girl should be playing soccer.' I went back to my team and said, 'Brother Joe is not going to let me play,' and there was an uproar.

The boys arranged that I would get changed in the school bus, they would go and get changed in the change rooms and then we would be on the field. I would have my privacy, it was all worked out.

They went to Brother Joe, told him what the situation was, and it all worked out fine and I played. Can't remember what the score of the game was, but I can remember changing in the bus. From then on that was the end of school, so to speak, and it didn't really matter from then on because I had finished school and I was doing other things.

Another lasting impression from her time playing representative football in the early years was the inconsistency of the male coaches. However, the importance of male coaches that the women encountered early in their careers—many of whom were brothers and fathers—often helped to keep them in the game.

> As far as my club coaches were concerned, they were always dads. They were always fine because they were in it to help their daughters. Once in a while you were lucky enough to get someone who actually had some soccer knowledge that could teach you something new. My father coached a number of the teams that I played in, and he also coached a state team.

But when Theresa reached state and national representation, problems became apparent.

> I believe that a number of the male coaches that were coaching national teams at that particular point of time weren't in it for the good of the women's game, they were in it only for their own benefit. A lot of them thought that it might lead them to other jobs within the men's game.

Theresa believes many male coaches disadvantaged interstate players, favouring those from their state.

> There was a lot of inconsistency, and particularly if a coach came from a particular state there seemed to be a lot of bias towards those people from that state, and it wasn't due to the fact that there was no money to bring people into camp because we all paid for everything ourselves anyway. It was more that it was easier for them to see those people in their particular state and not have to worry so much about what else was out there.
> I know for a fact that in Queensland the number of women playing soccer was huge compared to anywhere else, particularly in regional Queensland. Far North Queensland had a competition in the very early days, and so did New South Wales. New South Wales country had a good regional competition as well. Those girls from those areas were generally not even looked at, specifically because the coaches were focused on the players from the cities. It

was only if you were really, really good and they couldn't ignore you that you seemed to actually get into the national team.

The inconsistency with coaches continued right up until the end of Theresa's career.

> I will say at the end of my career, Steve Darby was appointed the national coach and for some reason or other, I don't think Steve every really considered me as a national player. I don't know why. He didn't really approach me or talk to me, and I felt that my career came to an abrupt end simply because he was appointed into the position, and he was very focused on Sydney-based players. I have a bit of regret as to the end of my career. I still think I had a couple of years left in me, but then, that's me – I'm probably biased about my own career. Maybe he was correct.

Despite some negative impressions of her time with the national team, Theresa holds close many fond memories of some male coaches who positively influenced her playing career.

> On saying that now, some of the national coaches were absolutely wonderful and have done a heap of work in promoting the women's game. Fred Robbins from Queensland was my first national coach, and I'm still in contact with Fred now. He was a pioneer and was in it for all the right reasons. He just wanted to see the development of the world game for females. Jim Selby, who was heavily involved in football, and who is still involved now, and has been his whole life. In the early years, I believe Jim was there to assist; he wasn't there for his own personal gain. He could see that women needed some assistance and some help, and basically, he was there to help us out. Others include Mick Hoar (Betty's husband) and Jimmy Southern.

1999, the year after Theresa left the game, saw considerable organisational changes. The amalgamation of Football Federation Victoria (FFV) and the Victorian Women's Soccer Association (VWSA) was underway as many of the country's women's associations began to hand over the running of their organisations to the state federations.

> Instead of finishing and walking away from the sport, I got involved in the administration and development side.

> At this particular point in time, which is 1998/1999, I was part of Women's Soccer Victoria, as the Development Officer—small little organisation that we had. In 1999, there were 65 open-aged women's teams in Victoria. When women's soccer got to this point, all the administration were volunteers and we got to a point where we were going to introduce junior girls' teams into the equation. Administratively, we just did not cope. Everybody was part time: the secretary was part time, the treasurer was part time. There were already 65 women's teams, and so it was a big organisation for it to be a voluntary organisation with no administration.
>
> The only person that was paid was me, and that was to do with the grant that we received. That was paltry pay, which only paid for my phone bills, basically, for all of the work. I didn't care because I could see that there was progress, and I was so involved and I loved it. It didn't even occur to me that it was not the thing that you did. What happened was the funding the funders who were then told, it was Vic Health or Diabetes Australia, that to get any more funding we should amalgamate into one body in Victoria. So we had to amalgamate with the boys. It was all put to the clubs.

Many opposed the move. Women had done so much to secure their autonomy, and few wished to relinquish the future of their sport to the male-dominated federations.

> People weren't happy. From my memory, we had a meeting at Richmond Soccer Club. I really was never interested in politics in the sport. I can't see why politics has to be involved in sport. I just wanted, okay, if we need the money, let's do this. Let's go forward, how bad can it be, we will have someone to do our books, you guys won't have to stress about it, you can get involved in other areas. I was pretty much all for it. But very naïve at that particular point in time because I always look at people and try to find the goodness in everything. It was put to us that it was an amalgamation, but really it was just a takeover.

Theresa passionately expresses the feelings of many women who had so tirelessly worked to get their game to where it was in the late 1990s. Many were sceptical, frightened and worried about where the sport was going and how it would be treated under the jurisdiction of the much larger and male-driven federations. More importantly, they feared that the voices of the many dedicated women who had dared to be different and strive for acceptance in a men's sport would be lost.

The women spoke strongly about the importance of recognising the pioneers and that a history of the women's game needs to include all women who have been involved in the development of the game at all levels and should not be restricted to the elite.

> It was very much pushed on us by everyone, and I was really annoyed at the time. We were women. We have done this, you haven't, and now you are going to take all the glory and all the funding for this wonderful thing from all of us (that) a women's body has done and make it your own.
>
> Even today, I get very angry when people don't recognise the struggle and the heartbreak that went into forming and producing and growing that association. That we all put in so much time and effort, and they just write it off as if football now started in the year 2000.
>
> Let's not forget that prior to that, most of the women's national players who were Victorian-based paid for everything themselves. It was through sheer dedication to the sport that they became who they are and that the reason you play sport in the first place is not purely for financial gain. We play sport for the love of the game, and that it is where my motivation came from and continues to come from.
>
> It is not about me, it is about us. That is why I get angry when I hear about ... It's not about, 'Look what I have done for the sport,' it is about what the sport has done for me, and I wouldn't be who I am if it wasn't for the people and the acquaintances and friendships and the situations that I have been in along the way. So I have high admiration for any women in soccer that have a small part to play. Everybody should be recognised today.

It was during this period, when Theresa's workload and concern over the future of women's football was at its peak, that she had to take some leave from football.

> I just wanted to make sure that what we had worked hard to achieve, that the history was recognised and that the work we achieved was recognised and that they built on that from then on. I was so passionate about that happening that I ended up having a breakdown, and my husband told me. I don't quite understand how it all worked myself because I didn't see that there was anything wrong, but he told me that this is what was happening.
>
> By this time, I had two young children, and a couple of months in(to) the whole process my husband was stabbed in an armed hold-up! I am always

> quite positive in my approach to things. I didn't think there was anything wrong. I thought I was taking care of everything, him included, and yes, I was, but I had run myself into the ground.
>
> After a lot of discussion with him, we decided that it was time for me to leave soccer for a while and let it get on with itself because I needed to take care of myself before anything else. That was early 2000.
>
> My involvement with FV then pretty much finished. What I did do then was just focus on my family and myself and had pretty much a complete break from football for a number of years, even though I knew what was going on and I listened and learned. That was the break that I needed and enough to allow me to come back after looking after my family and get back involved in the last few years and really enjoy it as much as I ever did.

During this time, the federal government commissioned the Crawford Report in 1999 (released in 2003), which majorly impacted how football was to be structured into the future. And this included the women's game. The smaller women's associations were required to amalgamate with the larger federations, and Victoria was one of the early state associations to hand over their operations. By 2001, there were only four left. In 2004, the ASF became the FFA, and the women became part of the individual state federations. Theresa was Development and Project Officer for female participation with FFV during this.

> But we did manage to survive the whole process. For me to go and still be employed by VSF, which is now FV, to go across and tell them what we had been doing and still be part of it and share the history and my knowledge on what had happened. We managed to keep that position, even when I finished, open. Nicky Leitch came in after me then it was Julie Ryan. We managed to keep a woman-only person in there. The first couple of years I worked at FFV, I worked with Ian Greener and Leslie Burrows. They were, particularly Ian, hugely understanding on where I was coming from. They were very happy working with me and introducing the right league structure and the right development programs, and to try and keep a history that we had developed going along without it being a total muscle takeover.

Theresa's playing time spanned 26 years, but she has never really left the game. Since handing in her gloves, she has been involved with FFV and is currently a valued member of the FFV Women's Standing Committee. Theresa currently supports women and girls' player development, coaching and the formation of Women's National Premier League (WNPL) clubs in Victoria. In recognition of her lifelong devotion to the development of women's football, Theresa was inducted into the FFA Hall of Fame in 2003 and the FFV Hall of Fame in 2011, becoming a life member of the latter in 2015.

> I always put myself in a position where I like to show people what a woman can do. If I am a role model as a woman, then you tell me what I can't do and I will show you what I can. There are definitely people there that will say, 'No, you can't do this' as a woman, or they put obstacles and barriers up. I don't generally think nowadays that is men's thinking. I think that is an individual's way of getting what they want. I don't call myself a feminist. I just think I am who I am. I don't think of myself as male or female. I just think of myself as me.
>
> Now I look back at it and I would never change anything because I travelled the world with my sport. I have got great memories and great friends. But it was hard. I sometimes think today, 'How the hell did I do that?' When you are younger, anything is possible.

4. Vicki Bugden

It's just our life, you know; our friendships and everything come from soccer.

A founding member of the women's team for the Richmond Rovers Soccer Club in Lismore, Vicki Bugden has dedicated her and her family's life to the women's game on the far north coast of NSW.

At the age of 12, Vicki became part of the first dedicated competition for women on the far north coast joining only three other clubs in 1974. Vicki was one of the first women selected in representative football for the far north coast when in 1976 she travelled to Queensland to take part in a football carnival and later was selected to represent Northern NSW in the state championships in Perth in 1977.

Vicki became a life member of the Richmond Rovers Football Club and has been involved as a player, coach and administrator. She is still to this day volunteering as the junior registrar/president and can be found most days at the clubhouse in Lismore.

The first recognised football competition for women on the far north coast of NSW was in 1974, when a local team, the Lismore Richmond Rovers Soccer Club, entered one with three other foundation clubs. The competition largely comprised high school girls, college students and those with brothers, sons, husbands or partners involved in the game. Indeed, the average age of the players was 13. Yet from this unassuming start, a women's footballing dynasty was born: Richmond Rovers have had one team in the top division of the competition up until recent years—the only women's team to do so.

Yet this journey began with challenges. Many women had tried to enter the game as juniors at first, but the male association rules prohibited them. They played on a Sunday afternoon at the Italo Stars grounds in Lismore, but little support came from local clubs, with the women having to buy and, in some cases, make their own uniforms.

It was onto this emerging scene that Vicki Bugden arrived in 1974, aged 12. Her family had moved to Lismore from Newcastle in 1963, and her brother introduced her to the sport following his own involvement with the Richmond Rovers. Little did he know at the time, but she would go on to pioneer the women's game on the far north coast of NSW.

> My brother signed up for Rovers in 1966, 67 from primary school. I had to sit with him while he trained, and then my mum would pick us up. I used to think that it was unfair that I could play in the backyard with everybody in the street but couldn't play out there. So he was a goalkeeper, and I used to stand beside the goals and, being my little brother, I used to run out and kick the ball out if it was going in, so in the end they used to tell me to go away.
>
> It wasn't until I was 12. I played netball and there were just some girls saying, 'I'm going to soccer training on Tuesday night,' and I said, 'You're what?' They said, 'I'm going to soccer training.' I was really reserved, really quiet and I was unsure, but as soon as the word soccer came up, I lost that. So Rovers was where Crosier Oval is now, that's where their field was, and I turned up there Tuesday night and I still remember the coach at the time said, 'Are you good enough?' I said, 'I just want to play,' and he said, 'No, are you good enough?' At this stage there were only four teams in the competition, and he was asking, you know, I thought that was a bit crazy, so anyway I got in and went from there.
>
> I was in second form at school and basically that team at Richmond Rovers had the majority of Richmond River High School kids. They all got involved because their brothers played or their boyfriends, so that's how that came about.

Vicki's parents were key supporters of their children playing sport, and went as far as buying the family home adjacent to the local football fields. The support enabled Vicki to become involved in football and to stay in the game long term. However, it wasn't long until Vicki noticed a certain stigma attached to the sport. Despite being unaffected by it, she realised women who played football were often perceived as lesbian. This was a common association with women who were involved in male-dominated sports during this period. How society has changed.

> At first, Mum and Dad would say we can't play soccer, and then living across the road we were always there. It would be a race to go and play over there before the council took the nets down and all that sort of stuff. Mum and Dad always knew that I just loved the game, so there was no, what would you say,

negative vibes from that side. But there was a stigma mainly because there was just a small group in other sports that had a stigma attached to them as far as homosexuality and whatever ... remember, this was the 70s.

I didn't really care about that, but yes, it came across to us that if you played you had to be butch, but I liked the game so much I didn't care. But as I got older, when I got to about 16, I sort of started to think, 'Oh, I wonder if that's how they do see us,' but as most of our team had boyfriends, our team didn't cop it as much. But it was definitely there, and I think it did turn a few people off, but they just thought it was a male sport, and females still were perceived as needing to just stick with stereotypical activities for girls. At school, girls weren't allowed to do metalwork, woodwork, etc. So you can see the stigma that existed.

The original Richmond Rovers clubhouse was where the Workers Club is now, and Mum and Dad, they actually bought the house across the road from the soccer field so that they didn't have to drive us to sport and everything. (Laughter.) We just walked everywhere. I think it was 1980 when we moved out here, East Lismore. But yeah, we've just always been with them, my brother has, Dad was actually the coach of the first girls' team. He was a rugby league player, so he had no idea but at least he got them together.

Vicki found that the male players at the club fully supported the women's teams and formed strong social bonds with them.

The fellas were always supportive of the girls. It was like they'd have their game on a Saturday and we'd go and watch them and like it was a big, you know social event. You'd have 40 people, it was a real club thing. Then the fellas would all go out. Everything shut at 12 then, but they'd have hangovers and the first thing on Sunday they'd go and watch women's soccer at nine o'clock with their pie and coke. It was a great atmosphere then. It still is now, but the men and the women supported each other big time in the club.

The local Rous Hotel was a great location for the club to meet and build on the camaraderie, which was important to the women and girls who played football. They just wanted to have fun. Playing the game was more about being carefree and being part of a team, and the social benefits of playing were a huge drawcard.

Winning a grand final in 1984, two goals to one in extra time. Going through undefeated, and the Rous Hotel said if we went through undefeated they'd put on a keg for us. We went down, but they didn't give us the keg, but they gave us wine and whatever, and I remember being very sick and all the players dancing on the tables.

The camaraderie was just great at the Rous. After training we'd go to the Rous and then Fridays, we'd all meet at the Rous again. Then Saturdays, we'd go after the boys' game, and then Sunday we'd be sitting on the front steps because the pub didn't open till 12 to go back in again. Often, we weren't drinking, it was just sitting and playing pool, even in summer—that's where everyone headed back to from the beach so we stayed as a big group, they were good times. So it's always been a thing for years after Cyndi Lauper's song, 'Girls Just Want to Have Fun'. Whenever we went to the Rous, we always hit that first and the boys would all go, 'Yeah, yeah, we get it, we get it.'

Way back when we first started, we were over at Italo Stars grounds on Sunday afternoons. After the competition increased, the games were moved to East Lismore. We used to play there because everyone could fit on these three fields. So we'd have games from nine a.m. right through, and that was a fantastic atmosphere.

Like so many of the pioneers, Vicki faced discrimination at the hands of the male-dominated clubs, which often made it difficult for women to play the game. The attitude of referees didn't help the situation, but if you wanted to play you had to abide by the rules whether you agreed with them or not. The ruling association refused to recognise women as important. 'It's only women's football' is the phrase often expressed by those in authority who place little importance on women in football.

The referees didn't see us as serious compared with the men's. The referee appointments weren't important, you know. It was just, we'd get referees that just stood in the centre and never moved—so we were down the list as far as getting referees. In the first few games, we used to have to line up and the referee would go and run his finger down everyone's back to see that we all wore bras and all that sort of stuff. I don't think men ever got checked whether they wore undies, but we had to wear bras. (Laughter.) That was just a thing.

I think it was in everyone's mind: 'Well, if that's what we have to do to play, that's what we have to do.' But the pregnancy issue was a big thing. If you knew you were pregnant and playing, the association couldn't put that in a clause because that was discrimination. It was advised strongly that you don't play and then the opposing teams, if they found out that someone was pregnant, they didn't want to play them.

In 1976, the first representative team from the FNCWASA travelled to Southport for a football carnival.

> The girls all decided, oh, there was a carnival in Southport, we might go up to that. They gave us the wrong starting time and we missed the first game, but we still came runners-up and our name got out then as the Lismore Girls. The only reason we lost one-nil was the team we played against were allowed to stack the team. We ended up playing the South Queensland state side, so we only lost one-nil. So our reputation got out and then, the next year, Queensland invited us up to Oxley, I think it was, for state selection and seven of us got in. By the time we got back, we got a phone call to say we couldn't be affiliated with South Queensland. Then we had to go to Newcastle, Warners Bay, and three of us got picked: Debbie Wraight (now Casey), Nell McMillan (now Perry) and myself, Vicki Klaus (now Bugden).

Being selected to play representative football was one thing but paying for it another, since the women received little to no support from the clubs or association.

> When we went away, we got very little from the club. We'd have to buy our own shorts and like. The boys, if they went away for rep, you know, they got the whole lot. We may have got one pair of shorts, that was all. We actually made our own uniforms: they were the school blouses, and we took the collars off and we took the buttons off and we put the black binding around here and put the RR on the pocket. We paid 30 cents a week to play, so that was to the refs so, yeah, interesting. Annelle Ambruster, a Rovers life member and our school's needlework teacher at the time, did the work.

The women often relied on fundraising to play, with the infamous lamington drives commonplace. Vicki has some fond memories of those times.

> We were a bit worried because Callan McMillan would say, 'Can we make pink ones?' and Mum would say, 'God, can we just get the chocolate ones done!' Then we were worried because they were in shirt boxes and someone happened to say, 'Did we get all the pins out of the shirt boxes?' And it was like, 'Too late now, most of them are gone,' and that was hilarious. That was really a fun time. We did a lot of fundraising to get away.

We had an old-time dance at McKees Hill, and the band always had a supper. The word got around that there was a supper, but there were only a few plates for the band and people were just scoffing this food and everyone started yelling—bring out the lamingtons!

After injuring herself playing basketball and being sidelined for six weeks, Vicki went to an Australian camp at St. Gregory's in Sydney in 1978. However, the pressures of representative football on a young woman from Northern NSW convinced Vicki to stay playing at a local level. The decision to head to Teachers College and having gained part-time work was the decider—finances ruled everything.

> That was interesting. We had an Australian possible versus probables game—that was quite overwhelming. It was at Marconi, and just the crowds, and I thought my gosh, what is this? I asked to come off. I didn't handle it very well at all. In Perth in 1977, I remember a German fellow from Western Australia. He happened to say to me, you know, 'Stick it out because I think by the time 1983 comes around, you'll be in the Australian side.' I thought that was a joke, but my ambitions weren't there. I just wanted to play and make sure women and girls played, so yeah, it was interesting times.
>
> When we went to Sydney in 1978, women's soccer was so much bigger down there. We were country bumpkins, you know, whatever they said must be right, and I didn't like where it was heading. If I could have just played for the sake of playing and just gone home afterwards or had the camaraderie like maybe the Australian Cricket Team had. I don't know, but I didn't like what I saw.

This feeling was again rekindled years later when Vicki was part of the Lismore liaison team for the Matildas versus France match at Oakes Oval in Lismore in 2001.

> Just to hang around the Australian side down at Ballina, and I was really pleased I never went any further. I don't think I would have liked it. I just didn't like the atmosphere around it and, like, I was there when they were eating and they had to watch absolutely everything they ate, and they were all virtually in the sin bin because someone ate half a Mars bar on the bus, and they were determined to find out who it was. So they were all in so much trouble because someone ate this Mars bar, and it was all false.
>
> I think that's what I don't like, it's all, they're sitting around together—I just sort of sat back and was watching, and they're all sitting around, 'You're

my best buddy, and I love you,' and all this sort of stuff. But they disliked each other with a vengeance because they're all playing for each other's spot, so the camaraderie isn't there in the top levels. That's probably an overgeneralisation, but at club level that's what it's all about. This higher level is all about you. It's sad, but I suppose that happens in every sport. But I was just taken aback, and I thought, I'm so pleased my kids never wanted to pursue it any further either.

Vicki was married in in 1983 and decided to again play representative football the following year. She continued to play and coach throughout her life until she finally hung up the boots in 2011.

I went back into the midfield, and it was a bit different—enjoyed that thoroughly. My husband at that stage was coach, but then after that I started breeding. Our first child came along in 1985, and the last in 1996. If I wasn't pregnant, I played, and when I was pregnant, I was coaching. There's only been one year since 1974 that I haven't played or coached and that was in 2007, but I was still doing the registrations here. It's been my whole life basically.

After having an eight-year break from the game in 2002, Vicki decided to make a comeback when her daughters were playing. She played her last game in 2011.

2002 was the last time I actually played on the field, and I had an eight-year break and then I came back. My two daughters were playing, and I played in goals and I found that really hard. (Laughter.) Really hard because a lot of people that only knew my name would want to sit and watch me put my boots on and all that sort of stuff, and I just thought no. I was hitting 50 and I was only playing out there if they were short of a goalkeeper. It was fourth division, and the girls were playing. When I had that last game there was no sadness or anything. I thought, no, this is it, it's time to go.

The ground was too hard, like it didn't hurt that much before (laughter) but when I hit the ground this time it hurt. So, yeah, I knew that it was, who was it that said—Wayne Pearce (international rugby league player)—'better to retire a year too early than a year too late!!' That always stuck in my mind. Just too hard on the body. I didn't like it when my body couldn't do what it used to do, no, so, depressing.

Vicki helped administer the game from the very beginning of the FNCWASA in 1978. The association remained in place until it amalgamated with Lismore District

Association Football Inc. in 1996. Vicki was still volunteering for Richmond Rovers as the club registrar when we met in 2013.

> I was registrar then, I was 17, Dad was president, Mum was assistant secretary and it went on from that. I've always been registrar or something since 1978 and then I was always coaching. Yet I didn't really get into the administration side of Rovers until the FNC women's folded and joined the men's. I was coaching and playing though.

The game has played a key role in Vicki and her family's life. She was awarded a life membership with the FNCWASA in 1988, and with the Richmond Rovers Club in 2003.

> Yeah, the game is everything. Sometimes Brian and I used to think that we put soccer ahead of the kids. A lady saw us yesterday and she said she just always remembers when Brian was coaching, and I was playing, and the four little kids would be on a rug. She never knew how come they were so well behaved but found out later that Brian had bribed them with lollies. You know, if they'd sit there for a full half they'd get lollies, so I've never had to worry too much about them. They just tagged along. Our eldest one didn't start playing until she was 23, she was always the netballer. She would say, 'I'm not playing soccer, I was dragged around soccer from the day I was born.'
>
> I spent a lot of time at meetings when the kids were little, probably shouldn't have, but then I think that's what's made the kids and us who we are. Brian and I will often talk about it over a beer or something, and we'll say, 'Where would we have been without soccer?' You know, you look at our whole life, my bridesmaids I met in Perth, they were from Newcastle and we've kept that friendship since I was 16. All our bridal party were soccer players, so it's our life, I think. One day we might just ease up a bit.

Vicki and her family are still involved with Richmond Rovers today. Brian (Vicki's husband) is the Premier men's coach in 2021 and sets up the fields for the juniors on Saturday mornings as well as coaches one of his grandson's teams. Vicki is junior registrar/junior president. They have children and grandchildren playing. Rovers is family.

5. Janelle (Nell) Perry

The greatest legacy from the game for me is friendship and really good memories. We just had such fun.

Nell Perry was born in 1954 and grew up in Lismore. She was instrumental in organising and developing women's football on the far north coast of NSW. Alongside her boyfriend/husband Callan McMillan, founder of the Far North Coast Women's Amateur Soccer Association (FNCWASA) in 1977, Nell starred as a player with the foundation club Goonellabah—with Callan as coach. Nell was selected to play for Northern NSW in 1977 and travelled to Perth to compete in the national championships.

Just before Christmas in 1977 Callan tragically drowned and Nell lost all love of the game and left the playing field for 10 years before returning to play until the age of 45 in 1999. Football Far North Coast dedicated the Callan McMillan Memorial Shield in 1978 and Nell continues to be part of the presentation of the shield to the winning club in the pre-season competition.

Nell is a pioneer of the women's game on the far north coast of NSW and her dedication and love of the game lives on in the annual presentation of the Callan McMillan Shield.

While still in high school and several years prior to the official introduction of competitive women's soccer on the far north coast of NSW in 1974, Nell and some school friends wanted to get a couple of teams together and play games during lunch breaks and on weekends. Unfortunately, their parents disagreed and, despite loud arguments and pleas from the girls, quashed the idea.

> I was shocked at their reaction, as I had played every other sport—I was playing hockey at the time. I couldn't see how soccer was any more dangerous than that and basketball. I was really good at athletics, but couldn't play soccer apparently. I got cranky and so did they. (Laughter.) That didn't eventuate.

> That's why I didn't play then until I was old enough that they couldn't tell me what to do. They were only looking after my welfare. They thought soccer was just too rough, especially Mum, and heading the ball would do all sorts of damage. She just didn't want to know about it.

A few years later in 1973, Callan McMillan, Nell's then-boyfriend, who she would marry the following summer, decided to enlist the help of a few other enthusiastic locals and try to get a competition for women up and running.

Callan was the son of Scottish immigrants who had settled in Australia in 1972. His father, Callan Snr (Pa), had been known for his skills back in Scotland, and the family's enthusiasm for football provided Nell with the necessary support to become involved in the inaugural women's competition on the far north coast.

> I don't really know how the idea came up, but my father-in-law, who was Callan McMillan Senior, always played football in Scotland. He was a very good player. They just seemed to think it was a good idea to try and get a women's comp started in town. It was organised that we should have a trial match, if we could get enough girls together, over at Richmond River High and just see where it went from there. That's basically where it started.

The first game played in Lismore was a trial match held at one of the local high schools one Saturday afternoon in the winter of 1973. Its purpose was to not only gauge the interest from future players, but also community interest as well.

Nell remembers the match attracted a large crowd—not just the parents and friends of the players but many curious onlookers as well, mostly men who had come along to see if the girls could actually kick a ball.

> We must have done all right because they decided that they would put their heads together and see if they could get a comp running. Callan really pushed for it. This was in 1973.
>
> We chased around to find players for the teams. We ended up with three teams: Goonellabah, who I played for, Richmond Rovers and Italo Stars got a team together. I think it was basically word of mouth, 'Hey, go and ask all your mates if they want to play soccer' sort of thing, originally, and you needed so many girls, so you went round until you found enough for your team and a couple of reserves. That's how it kicked off, and then somebody made up a draw. We got to know each other pretty well as there weren't that many teams. (Laughter.)

Over the coming years more teams joined and by 1977 the competition had grown to 14.

While the women's game was growing, Nell still remembers instances that reinforced the view that football was a male game, and that women and football was a mix still to be settled. Those who ran the game often made decisions that trivialised the women's desire to play. Most clubs were only interested in the men's game and women who played football were often seen as a novelty, and generally not being capable enough to play the game.

> I remember our first games. We didn't even get to play with a real soccer ball. I guess they (the men) thought that a leather ball would be too heavy! We had to play with one of those plastic blow up balls, that were really light and with a breeze blowing and you kicked it high, you would spend the next half hour looking for it because, it just went. I hated that.

In the initial stages, the women only played 35-minute halves and continued to do so right up until about 10 years ago when it was increased to 45 minutes, the same as the men. The women's games were always played on Sunday because the men's competition used the grounds on Saturdays, and also each female player would pay a small amount towards a fee for the referees. The women had to provide their own shirts at first. The Goonellabah girls were a bit lucky in that the club gave them some old men's team shirts to wear. 'We didn't care ... we just wanted to play football!'

The men involved in the game remained uncertain as to how women and football would work.

> When we first started, I thought the men were a little, 'Well, we will see how this goes.' They were a bit sceptical. They didn't really knock us, they were just a bit sceptical; they didn't know how good girls could be.

Once the competition got going, the men supported the women and often attended games. It didn't matter either way to Nell.

> When I was playing for Thistles (Lismore-based soccer club) they always supported us. They would come and watch our games, and we would go and watch their games. I can't remember any real negativity from the fellows about us. Maybe other people would have different memories, different

experiences, but I have never been one to really let other people's opinions concern me that much. Unless it is somebody I really care about. As a general rule, if Joe Blow down the street doesn't like me or thinks I am an idiot, then he can think that. I am not going to lose any sleep over it. (Laughter.)

In 1976, the first representative team from the FNCWASA travelled to Southport for a football carnival.

We wanted soccer to grow, so we started playing competitions in South East Queensland. We played a couple of carnivals up there, and then we got in contact with the Northern NSW mob, and we were invited to bring a rep team down (together) and just see how we went. That first year we went down, Debbie, Vicki and I got picked for the Northern NSW side, which is pretty good.

As the competition expanded, Nell was soon to develop into a leading player. Her skills earned her state selection in 1977 and a trip to Perth for the national titles in August.

I can remember when we went over to Perth. It was all so exciting, it was such a big deal. Three little country girls off to play in the Aussie championships. I will always remember it. You just don't forget things like that. Winning the grand final was really neat as well. You play the grand final at Oaks Oval and that was big time here. Even then, men's teams would come and watch.

Women's football in the 1970s was less well supported than now, and the cost of a trip to Perth—which involved flights and a hotel—was a major obstacle for Nell and the others. Fundraising was again necessary. The support of family and friends was critical in keeping the women in touch with the football world.

The community were very supportive. We would hold stalls down the street. We went round different businesses and got them to donate prizes for raffles; they were good. We raised enough money, can't remember exactly how much it cost us now, or how much we contributed ourselves, but I am pretty sure that we raised the major part of what we needed.

We had lamington drives. They were always a big hit. We would go to Klaus's place after work or after training and make these flaming lamingtons. I am not joking, we were so sick of lamingtons. (Laughter.) I always remember

> Klaus's dog would sit under the kitchen table, and anything that would hit the deck, the dog got!! (Heavy laughter.) We made lots of lamingtons. We raised a lot of money.

The tyranny of distance was also a barrier.

> It was a pain to go to Newcastle all the time for training, but you did it. That is what you do. If you get into a team that is based down there, well you've just got to do it.
>
> We caught the train. We would go down on a Friday night after we finished work or school, and we would wait for the train. Catch the 11.00 train, and we would fall off the train the next morning and get our billets sorted out. People down there were fantastic, we all got billeted. You would have breakfast and a cup of tea and then you would be down the soccer fields. This is Saturday—competition started Saturday afternoon, and you went Sunday and then back on the train Sunday night. You get home Monday morning, and you go to work or school. You did it. I couldn't do it now. I was a lot younger then.

Just before Christmas in 1977, Callan tragically drowned trying to save a young girl. Nell lost the husband she loved, her mentor, the person who had encouraged her to play the game and the man whose enthusiasm had nurtured her early career. She was re-selected for the Northern NSW state team in 1978, but her heart was no longer in it.

> I stopped playing the year after Callan died. We had been to Perth for the Aussie championships in the August, and he died in the December.
>
> I kept playing. I went down to Newcastle with the girls for state selections. I got selected again and then we would have to go down to Newcastle for training every second weekend, and in between that I was playing basketball.
>
> After Callan died, I lost the love of it. It just wasn't the same. I still liked the game, it just wasn't the same without him. He used to coach our club side, and coached our rep side, along with Pa. Pa would be at every training session, and he would take a bunch of girls and do drills, then Callan would take another bunch and they would share the workload. Pa always came to Newcastle with us, then Callan was just gone.
>
> I went down to Newcastle this weekend to train, knowing that I was going to pull out of the team, but I wanted to do it in person because I had

made good friends down there with the coaches and the people that were associated with soccer.

Nell's tragic loss robbed her of her way of life, leading her to leave her hometown and the game for 10 years.

> I really enjoyed it obviously when Callan was alive. That's what we did every week, several days a week. That's where we were, soccer. As I said, it wasn't until after Callan died that it just stopped meaning the same thing to me anymore.
>
> I was just a player. That's what I wanted to do. I just wanted to play. I didn't want to be any official or anything like that. I didn't mind doing the raffles and getting businesses to donate prizes. But I'm not the type of person who would then devote the rest of my life to a club. I am really glad there are people like that out there, because where would we be? But I don't think I am one of those persons. I was registrar for a little while, for the local competition, but then I stopped playing and I wanted to get away from it. I did, I didn't go near it for years and years.

The football community rallied to support the family, and the Callan McMillan Shield was presented as a memorial to a great pioneer of the game in 1978. The shield has been a major part of the women's competition since its inception and is currently presented to the winning team of the Far North Coast Football women's pre-season competition.

> Callan had been so active in getting the local association up and running with all the effort he put in at training. He would go to club training, rep training, state training, and he never missed a session. Plus he played as well, so he would have his training as well, and I think that is why it came about. Ma and Pa thought it would be nice. I don't even know who came up with the original concept of the McMillan Memorial Shield. I just know that it came to be, and that Ma and Pa donated the shield. From the first humble beginning it has grown from there. It is an ideal situation to keep it running and use it as a pre-competition. That seems to always get a good following and good support—teams like it.

After a break of some 17 years, Nell returned to football and continued playing until age and injuries caught up with her. She eventually retired aged 45.

> After 17 years away from the game, I thought I would have another run—as you do! These were first division girls after not playing for 17 years! The first game nearly killed me. (Laughter.) The first game was down in Woodburn; it was hard work, but it was good.
>
> So then I played with Thistles for a couple of years in first division, then I had a run in second division because they were short of players. I went and fell in a hole and broke my ankle, so that put me out of the first division grand final. Then when I went back the following season, I thought, I don't want to play first division anymore. So then I went and played second division. The second stint was probably the same length of time as the first stint, about four years.
>
> I was getting a bit old, the fields were getting longer and you don't recover quite as well, and my knees were stuffed by that stage anyway. Time to call it quits, and I had other things to do.

Nell still has fond memories of the game. She is proud to be associated with the sport and of the role she and her husband played to kick-start the women's game on the north coast of New South Wales back in 1973. Football Far North Coast (FFNC) has continued to remember Callan and the effort he contributed to the game. In 2012, FFNC approached Nell and Callan's mother (Ma) and asked if they would present the shield to the winner of the women's pre-season competition in honour of his memory.

> I'm grateful that soccer as a sport in this area has chosen to continue to remember Callan and the effort that he contributed to the game. I really think it is terrific, and (at) this year's Callan McMillan and the year before, Ma and I have presented the shield and it is really quite nice. When they first asked me, I thought, do I really want to go there? It's not my life anymore. When I got down there, I was really glad I did.

Nell continues to present the Callan McMillan Shield each year alongside Ma and is hopeful 'that the history of women's soccer in this area isn't forgotten or underplayed.'

> The greatest legacy from the game for me is friendship and really good memories. We just had such fun. We used to really enjoy ourselves, that's what I remember about it. I don't remember any bitchiness. I suppose it

might have been around, but it went straight over me. I was just out there playing the game and having a good time. I really enjoyed it obviously when Callan was alive. That's what we did every week, several days a week, that's where we were, soccer. I still have friends from that first period of time when I played, and some of my closest friends now were generated from the second stint, when I played with Thistles. I see them quite a lot, several times a year and even more. Most of them are coming out here for a Christmas party in a week's time.

6. Dalys Carmody

When you are at a dinner, and you get your name read out that you made the national squad. You go and ring Mum and Dad up—it is pretty special.

Dalys Carmody began her playing career in the Shire—south of Sydney in 1977 at the age of 12. She went on to represent NSW in 1986 and 1987, and in 1989 was also selected to play for the national team.

Dalys came to the game during the formative years of international women's football—a time when players received little to no support and had to rely on family and fundraising in order for them to realise their football dreams. Her story is one which reflects on the hardships faced by the women who strived to play the game throughout this time.

While Vicki and Nell were making waves in Northern NSW, in a small suburb in the southern region of the state's capital, Sydney, another pioneer was getting her start. Dalys Carmody began her football career in the Sutherland Shire, known colloquially as 'The Shire'. She was born in 1964 and lived in Grays Point, which is located on the northern edge of the Royal National Park in southern Sydney. While Grays Point Soccer Club started in 1965, it didn't field a senior women's team until 1977 with the first junior teams following in 1978.

> I was in high school in Year 7, and I used to do Little Athletics with my friend Lisa and she said, 'Have you ever thought of playing soccer?' I said, 'Do girls play soccer?'—'Of course they do, why don't you come to training and have a look?' So I went and never looked back, loved it. I had a pretty good left foot and it started from there. Grays Point at the time didn't have a women's team so I played for Gymea Lillies, Gymea Bay. I started playing when I was 12.
>
> I played right through, had a couple of years off, but basically played from 12 through to 30, at a guess.

Dalys's family were football people and highly supportive, while friends recognised her talent early and predicted that one day she would play for Australia.

> My mum was a mum and Dad had his own business. Dad was a boilermaker, but when I started playing, they were really happy for me to play. My brothers played football, my younger brother, who unfortunately is not with us anymore, he was a very good goalkeeper. He played for Grays Point. When Grays Point actually got a women's team, I went back to play with them, and we were really successful. We won the competition for a lot of years—had a really good team.
>
> Everyone that I knew never turned their noses up. They were all supportive and at some point said, 'See that girl over there, she will play for Australia one day.' They were—everyone was fantastic.

Women's football began to grip nations worldwide in the 1970s. By the time Dalys first strapped on a football boot in 1976, regular women's competitions had been established in most states of Australia.

> Most of my junior career was in the Sutherland Shire, and then, when I was 16/17, they actually got a representative team together and I played for Sutherland. We had to travel to places like Kuringai and Bosley Park. Sutherland Shire had a federation, and we used to play at Kareela, which was their representative oval on Bates Drive.
>
> We had a lovely coach, Ron Tripp. He used to take as many girls as he could fit into his car as possible. We had to go out to Marconi, Parramatta and places like that. It was a long way, but you did what you did to play.

As so often happened in the developing years of women's football, the players had to move around different clubs in search of those which would best support them.

> Then we had to move to St George, and from there, teams folded as quick as they came because the administrative side put everything into their men's team, so we had to move on and find other ways. One year, I even came up and played with Newcastle. I played with Raymond Terrace, I think. A few of us car-pooled. We didn't have to go there to train, just to the games. Every second game we would go there and then have games in Sydney. We

didn't want to go to the strong teams like St George. We wanted to make it a competition, so if everyone went to the good teams, there was no point, it wasn't a competition then.

There were a few of us from the Shire that wanted to represent. We played with Sydney United for a couple of years. A Greek Club called Hellas ... were very supportive of us. They paid our registration, looked after us after the games. They had women's teams and very strong men's teams as well. Sydney United were another strong club. That was the Premier League for women's soccer—that's what they call it now. We used to call it first grade. There was first grade and then they had reserve grade for women, just the two grades. It was played separately to the men's. Sometimes, at Edensor Park, I remember we were with Sydney United, we would play the leg before the men's Premier League, which was good because there were quite a few people that would come earlier and watch the girls go round. We kicked off about 1.30 p.m. leading into the men's game, which kicked off about 3.30 p.m. They were really good to us.

From there we folded. They didn't have a women's team anymore. We had to look for a club that would take us in. After Sydney United, I went back to the Shire and played club football, because they had an over-35s competition there. It was good over-30s. You could put your hand up, it was like tag, there was no such thing as reserves. It was unlimited changes, as long as you went to the linesmen and swapped. I thought, this was fantastic when they brought that in. So I just played in an over-35s competition back in the shire—I played at Cronulla RSL.

The first national championships for women's football were held in August of 1974 in Sydney. After the inaugural championships, the tournament was held annually and in a different state each year.

> You went to tryouts—there was a coach and manager selecting a squad of 17 or 18 to represent NSW to go to the national trials. Then you got selected in the squad and from there they cut it down and picked the squad to go to the nationals. I did a couple of NSW tours before I got selected to play for Australia.

Dalys played for NSW at the national championships in 1986 in Adelaide, 1988 in Newcastle and in Canberra in 1989.

> When I got my first NSW jersey my first game was against Northern NSW, in Adelaide, at the nationals. I scored a nice goal, hit it sweetly just outside the 18-yard box, and I will never forget it. We won, we went through undefeated that year. We had a draw against South Australia in the last game. That was the only point we dropped. That's my most memorable, and I guess after the nationals, when you are at a dinner, when you get your name read out that you made the national squad, that is pretty special. You go and ring Mum and Dad up—it is pretty special. Those would be without a doubt my two favourite moments.
>
> 1989 was the year I got selected to play for Australia.

Australia hosted its first international event since 1979 when the third Oceania Cup was staged in Brisbane in 1989. Entries were received from New Zealand, Papua New Guinea, Chinese Taipei, Hong Kong, Polynesia and India. Unfortunately, Hong Kong, Polynesia and India withdrew. To avoid needing a bye, Australia entered separate Green and Gold teams. Dalys was selected in the Green team. Betty Hoar was manager, with her husband Mick as assistant coach.

> I didn't go far in my elite level, just to Brisbane. We stayed at the Olims Hotel, Storey Bridge. We had a week there and we trained at the QEII Stadium. So that was an intense week of training before we had the actual tournament. We played New Zealand, Papua New Guinea—they were always there, god love them, and Chinese Taipei; they were quite strong. They're the main ones I can think of.
>
> John Doyle. He was our coach. He had the girls for a couple of years. Actually, I thought he was a brilliant coach: very hard, but I learnt a lot from him. Only men coaches in my representative career, but then when I went back to club, there were women coaches. There was a Scottish lady; she came from a background playing in Scotland. Allan Lynton was another one. He was our coach for NSW, but apart from that, all men growing up in football. They were great, really good.

Australia's Gold and Green drew against each other; both lost to New Zealand and Chinese Taipei, and both defeated Papua New Guinea. Chinese Taipei went on to defeat New Zealand in the final 1–0.

The poor results caused an upheaval. They came not long after Australia's solid performance at the 1988 FIFA Women's Football Tournament in China, where the team defeated leading football nation Brazil 1–0. The lacklustre performance led Doyle to resign, with most agreeing that inadequate preparation time had led to the poor performances.

> There was one claim to fame. I think at one stage they beat Brazil and that was unheard of as we were a bunch of misfits. It was hard for the national team to train together because some were from Melbourne, some were from Canberra, Brisbane—all over the place.

While distance was a barrier to the development of the national team, the players also contended with inadequate financial support and resources.

> How sad is this: I remember, we got a little spray jacket and it had the coat of arms on it. It wasn't even sewn on; it was like a little badge and glued on with gold art line pen markers, Australia 1 (as there were two teams representing the Oceania), and it had Perry Park and just the dates on there with Oceania, and it was just this gold. I will never forget it. It wasn't even embroidered nicely or anything like that. Patrick sponsored us. I don't know if they are in business anymore. Our shorts were Patrick. We got a spray jacket and just our gear. That was it. I don't think we got anything else. There was no tracksuit.

The women had to pay for everything, even flights. And Dalys relied on her community to get to the Oceania Cup.

> How I got there, it didn't come out of my pocket. I played seven a side in a men's competition at Grays Point. Because I was a local there, I was the only girl they would let play. We used to have drinks after playing and the guys, they were businessmen, just passed the hat around. I was working for an importing company and my boss gave me a few things to raffle off. One guy got up on one of the chairs and announced, 'Dalys is representing Australia in the Oceania Cup. She has to come up with X amount of dollars, let's try and help her on her way, so she doesn't have to pay her own way.'
> I don't think I had to pay much at all. They just threw in $10 and $20 notes and helped me out. I was really lucky with the Grays Point community as a whole, they were fantastic.

While the community, family and friends were supportive, the women's game was still subject to ingrained discrimination and barriers to its development. Inhospitable playing schedules and the lack of access to suitable training facilities were still common practice at some clubs.

> Back when, we would play on a Friday night, in the middle of winter. Who would want to come and watch a Premier League game on the Central Coast at 7.30 at night? You've got to be joking, you wouldn't do it. Like, if I wasn't playing, I wouldn't be there. Whereas 2.30 p.m. on a Sunday afternoon is much more appealing than 7.30 p.m. on a Friday night. So things like that make all the difference.
>
> The Premier men would get, say, two thirds of the field, and we would have to train in this pokey corner. Why was that the case? Why couldn't we split that, even have a game together? But sometimes the men would say, 'No, no, we are not playing.' That was back then, but now we are in the 21st century, everything has changed. Now, the women would get half the field if that's what they want ...

The lack of recognition was also a major challenge for the women.

> People don't realise it comes out of their pocket. For them to travel and they give up a lot. Their hair would stand up on their heads if they realised. I could guarantee, the last World Cup, which was a Women's World Cup, and the girls got, I think to the quarters—I think Sweden beat them in the end. They would have been broke. They would have gone over there with hardly any money and hardly any support. A lot of people would not have a clue about them. I don't know if that is ever going to change. I think it is sad that a few of the girls had to go to the States to play because they have a league over there that the girls get a substantial amount of money (for playing in). It is sad that they had to go over there to play to earn a quid. It is just the way it is.

Things have changed since Dalys played football.

> A lot has changed, but still not near to what it should be. They get a little more (in) endorsements now. At least now they get a tracksuit, a kit bag, they might get a pair of boots. They might even get the emblem, (the) Australian Coat of Arms, embroidered on their little spray jackets now, that's a big thing.

FFA recently introduced the concept of the commemorative cap. Previous national representative players were presented with caps to recognise individual contributions to the national team and their role in women's football in Australia.

That was the first thing that Soccer Australia had ever done for us; actually, that was a real nice touch. That was before a double header in the Women's W-League and it was at Leichardt Oval. It was a pity they couldn't get everyone there. It was a nice reunion of some of the girls who played. They actually gave us a few drinks, a wrap—a little sandwich—nice salad. We never, ever got much from Soccer Australia.

There were no official photographers or anything like that—just from family and friends that were there. Julie Dolan presented me with the cap, which I was thoroughly happy about because in my eyes she is number one. She is probably the icon of women's soccer. Cindy Hayden is probably another one and another girl called Kim Lymbrick. They were just phenomenal players to me. She presented me with my cap. I was pretty chuffed about that.

I still keep in touch with the Queenslanders who I played against. Definitely made friendships out of it from the nationals in Adelaide, when I first represented, and still keep in contact with those people. We were up there for a 50th two weeks ago. I have made lifelong friends out of it. They will be in my life as long as I am around.

Dalys now lives in Lennox Head and works for a local sports store.

I currently work in a sports shop, some girls, young kids come in. I ask, 'Are you going to be the next Matilda?' And I don't like them saying it, (but) my bosses would say, 'One is serving you right now!' They would say, 'Ohhh, you played for Australia.' I don't like that because I don't feel representing for one year, to me doesn't cut it, but to these kids, 'That would be unreal.' Watching the game grow to where it is now, I would love to know the statistics of how many women are now playing in Australia. I probably would be blown away. Even to the extent, now when I watch Mel and the girls play, they've got quite a few teams, just up here in the Northern Rivers. They have three or four grades just in opens. For an area as small as we are up here, I find that fantastic.

Once you set your mind on something, if you really want it bad enough, you can achieve those goals. When I represented, (that was) one of the things that helped me out because we had a fitness program that we were given, that our coaches and managers wanted us to adhere to, and I was staunch with that. I probably trained extra and that paid off for me because I got in the A team. I probably didn't have the skill level of some of the other girls, but the fact that I was so fit, because I trained that much harder, that would be one thing. The old cliché: 'If you want something bad enough, you will get it.'

7. Deborah Nichols

If you could play football, they would talk to you differently, absolutely. They didn't see you as a girl, they just saw you as a footballer.

Deb Nichols has been involved in women's football since the age of 12. After migrating to Australia with her family in 1975 Deb went on to forge her career in the developing years of the Victorian women's competition, playing with several clubs.

Women's football in the 1970s was beginning to take hold in Australia; however, many obstacles to participation remained, foremost being a lack of support. Despite the hardships Deb represented Victoria at 10 national championships, winning three titles, and in 1988 was selected in the national team. Her dedication to her playing and coaching career over some 40 years is second to none, and she continues to give back to the game through her coaching in the WNPL.

Deb Nichols burst into the Victorian state women's competition in 1975 aged 12, joining the newly named club Springvale City (formerly Pegasus and Repco Clayton). She played for her home state of Victoria for over 20 years during the 1970s and 1980s and represented her country in 1988/89. A strong advocate for the women's game, Deb is a highly regarded member of the football community in Victoria. She is recognised as a pioneer in the development of the women's game and is currently coaching in the WNPL.

Deb was born in Hanover, Germany, in a British military hospital in 1964. She immigrated to Australia in 1975 at 11, following a short spell in a school team in England aged nine—until a rule change excluded girls from the game.

> First known picture of me, I am about knee-high to a grasshopper with a football in front of me. I think my old man wanted a boy first up, and I pretty much grew up with a football from the moment I could walk. I played school soccer in the UK, at a time when girls didn't normally play. We played one

year in the school team with boys, and then they brought in a rule that girls couldn't play with boys so I had to play the following year in netball, while the boys played football. It would have been 1973 or around that time.

Like many migrant families arriving in Australia at that time, football clubs provided a sense of community and a link to national culture. Deb's father was in the armed forces and keenly supported his daughter's passion, and she was soon rushed into the Springvale first grade side. Unknown to Deb, fellow football pioneer and later friend Theresa Deas had also begun her playing career at the same age some two years earlier with the Dandenong City Club.

When I came to Australia, I was in Springvale in the Enterprise Migrant Hostel. There were fellow Brits and Irish. Someone said, 'There is a women's football team down at Springvale City, why don't you go there?' I was only 12 years old. I had only just ever played with the boys. So I went down there, and that was when women's football wasn't in age groups. There was no junior women's football. I started at Springvale in 1977 as a 12-year-old in open age. I played there for about six years and then the team folded.

Such a mix of ages was common in the early years of women's football as teams struggled for numbers, with pre-teen girls often pitting themselves against women in their 30s in open teams.

In my first game, I got kicked up into the air in the first 30 seconds—welcome to football! (Laughter.) I hadn't played with or against adults. You look back, there were no shin pads, and the pitches were mud pits. But I really enjoyed it.

Family, friends and work fully supported Deb's early involvement in football, which she attributes to her father's encouragement:

Must have been my old man (laughter). It was a given—Mum and Dad would drive me wherever I needed to go and play. Mum just got used to the fact that I would stay in bed for a week crook but could drag myself out of bed to go and play football, and then come home and go back to bed! They just got used to it. That's the way it was.

Mum used to always come and watch. Maybe the theory was that at least they know what you are doing and keeping out of trouble and enjoying it. I

> think she knew she could never stop me. I used to go and kick a ball at school, play all day at school then come home and kick a ball again. I think she knew it was a lost cause from day one to ever try and attempt to stop me playing.

The women also needed their employers' support to stay in the game, particularly if they were playing in state and national representative teams, which often required the players to travel.

> Work was really supportive. I commenced full-time work at Telstra (then Telecom Australia) in 1983, and they gave me leave without pay—now you get elite athlete leave. They never knocked me back when I needed to play, so work was very supportive. Even now with my coaching commitments, they are still very supportive; they are flexible with what I need to do.

Not all women received the amount of support needed to train and play weekly. Child support was virtually non-existent, for example. This is an issue still debated today, and still a major barrier to women participating in football. Some of the women found that motherhood provided additional challenges, especially if no support was forthcoming from partners to enable them to train and play, while the men were not always subject to the same type of issues. The role of a supportive partner then becomes paramount for staying in the game long term. Some did not have a choice, while others had to make the hard decision between a family, a career or playing football.

> Maybe some that played in teams—maybe had partners or husbands that didn't support them playing, especially if children came along and they weren't so helpful in allowing that person to get to training. We can't get them to look after the kids so they couldn't get to training. You have to have buy-in from everyone. If it was the other way around, they would go to training and wouldn't worry about the kids.
>
> I would say this was a while ago, not recently. I have got players that play in my reserve team that have kids and it is pretty much the husbands are on board or, if they are not, they were never going to get there in the first place. Most women were playing when they met their partners, and it's like, 'I'm going to do this, if you don't accept me doing this ...' A bit of respect. The world has changed.

With family and work supporting her, Debbie could continue her club football, which included playing stints with Springvale, Dandenong and Berwick City. When I interviewed her, Deb was at the Sandringham Club.

> I then went to Dandenong North. This is where it gets complicated because Dandenong North then became Dandenong. We then moved the team to Berwick City, then to what is now Casey Comets, but was originally Cranbourne Soccer Club. I was involved with them from 1983 to about two years ago (2010). I am now coaching at Sandringham. So that is my club football.

While playing for Casey Comets, Deb was selected to play for her state and went on to play in 10 national championships, winning three titles in 1987 (Alice Springs), 1989 (Canberra) and 1992 (Brisbane).

> I played in the Victorian squad for nearly 20 years in the open age, again no age groups. Up until about in my mid-30s.

Then in 1988, Deb got her shot on the international stage, debuting for Australia at the pilot World Cup in China. According to tour manager Elaine Watson, the highlight of the preliminary rounds was defeating Brazil in the opening match.

> Obviously, my debut (...) was pretty memorable. I played for about two years. I didn't play a lot of nationals in those days. Not as many as they play now. I think I made my debut and played for Australia for about 12 caps.

In 1989 Deb was selected to play for the Australian Green team in the third Oceania Cup held in Brisbane, and later that year for the Prima Cup tour to Japan in which Australia remained undefeated. In 1991 Deb was part of the Australian team selected to compete in the Oceania Qualifying Tournament for the first FIFA World Cup for women. Unfortunately, Australia failed to qualify after losing to New Zealand.

> Overall, I didn't stop playing officially until three years ago. My surgeon said that I had to stop playing! But recently, I have filled in a couple of times in reserves when my goalkeeper got injured. (Laughter.)

While most women reported experiencing discrimination throughout their playing careers, Deb was one of the few to play with clubs that supported women's football.

> From my own experiences, I have been probably—shouldn't say fortunate, shouldn't have to say that—but I think we have had a lot of respect in the clubs I have been involved with. I have noticed a lot of other clubs that don't get the same support even today, and they are treated very much as second class. And until the FFV really stepped in and started insisting that Women's Premier League be played on a certain pitch, like the No. 1 ground, you would go to games where the U/14 boys would take precedence to the women. They would be shoved out the back park.
>
> When it comes up, and it did maybe four years ago when we had an incident at a club, where they wanted to play the boys game and shift us to the small crappy pitch—and it was funny because we hadn't seen that kind of thing for so long. We took for granted that everyone accepted the women as equals, but it was a right bum fight that day to get the girls playing on the main pitch. At some clubs, it's still women down below junior boys. But I am fortunate. The clubs I have been involved in have treated the girls the same. There are the men's and there are the women's, and all the juniors come under them. I have been very lucky, I think, because I know some people who don't have that fortunate experience.

The rare club that provided an even playing field for all players often enabled women to develop positive relationships with administrators, coaches and male players.

> I got along really well with all the club people at Casey Comets. I was there for 15 years, and they were very supportive of women's football. I didn't have any head-butting moments. We were probably one of the clubs that had an equal relationship. We had very supportive presidents that helped, which isn't so predominant maybe in some other women's football clubs.
>
> We got on really well with the male players as well. We used to train on the same night as the senior men, so we would catch up afterwards. They would come and watch some of our games or the girls would go and watch some of their games. I got on really well with all the coaches that coached the senior men. They were always up for a chat. Sometimes the girls would join into some of their sessions for cross training.

However, some of the positives were hard-earned. While the game has reached a level where access to participation and the rights of women to play have improved, a level of discrimination remains.

There will always be roadblocks, and there will always be people in there for their own gain. I have seen that over the years; people get involved for certain reasons, some people get involved to give something back to the game. Other people get involved to leapfrog from it and use it as a start. I have had some fun and games with some people, but it is part and parcel of it all.

Probably when you went back to the early days it was so different. Football has only been here for 40 years, and with girls playing, they used to look at us sort of sideways and ask, 'Why are you playing that?' Now, there are so many girls playing. You have so many girls wanting to play football. I see that massive change in mindset, that it is a good sport for girls to be involved in. I think that comes from exposure on TV, international competition. But to see parents encouraging the girls—it is no longer seen as a butch-type sport. It is seen as a good team sport, as an option to netball. I have seen a lot more support for it than there used to be.

Like Theresa Deas and other prominent women players, Deb found that if you had talent, the male players treated you differently and respected you.

I was probably lucky because I was a half-decent footballer, and I played in boys' teams, and right from knee-high to a grasshopper I could well and truly hold my own in any boys' team. So you certainly have respect. Peer respect. This person is a good footballer, so I had the confidence to, if someone said anything, I could quite happily put him or her back in their place.

We used to play against—going back to the state team with the girls—we used to play against mixed teams or men's teams, and we used to love it. They used to go, 'These girls can play, and they're fair dinkum.' You earned respect through the years playing against certain teams.

If you could play football, they would talk to you differently, absolutely. They didn't see you as a girl, they just saw you as a footballer. I would never say they would beat me at something. It would just make me more determined to prove that I was as equal if not better than them.

I can be an obnoxious bastard when I want to!

The clubs also showed respect to teams that were winning and bringing them kudos.

We were a good club side. That side went 10 years of winning the championship, so we had huge respect wherever we went. I think the fact we had

> respect, and I played with—there were three or four international players in that club side, so most of the time, that club side was the best side in that club, and the club realised that and used to run off the publicity that that side generated in the local paper. We would be put in the paper whether it was Berwick City or Casey Comets. We were put up in lights, and the clubs realised that was worth tacking onto.
>
> With Berwick, we won the championships seven years out of seven for that club. We were well known. We won club, state tournaments and they definitely went, 'This is something we can benefit from!' And at Casey, which was Cranbourne, we were for the first eight years we were there, when that generation was still playing, we were the top side in Victoria.

But while a supportive club helped the women to be recognised and valued, being in the national team was often a different story. Women's sport during the 1970s was of little interest to most and received minimal media attention. Women in sport were often on their own and had to provide for themselves. This situation sometimes resulted in the situation where the best were not always selected for representative honours as only those that could afford to pay or had parents willing enough to pay for them could play.

> When I played internationals, you didn't get any coverage. No one knew who you were from a brass razoo. You could walk back through the airport with the World Cup, and they wouldn't know who you were. What they get now is fantastic.
>
> When I used to play international, we would contribute to our costs and for every state tournament in those 20 years we had to pay for ourselves. That would be the only thing where we were treated differently, because if the men went away for an international, they certainly wouldn't have paid.

After finishing her playing career in 2009, Deb stayed involved in the game through several coaching roles. Since then, she has become head coach of Casey Comets and was a senior coach with the Sandringham Women's WPL team. She has been twice voted as the WPL Coach of the Year by her peers and spent time as the assistant coach with Victoria Vision in the former Women's National League, which later became the W-League in 2008. In recent years, Deb has coached Southern United in the WNPL.

To honour her contribution to the development of women's football, particularly coaching and nurturing young girls in football, Deb was inducted into the FFV Hall of Fame in 2014.

> I have been involved since I was 12 years old. Through most of my club adult life until now, I didn't know anything else really. I can't imagine not being involved. Obviously, when you get older, it is tiring. Now it is so much more professional than what it was. There is so much more expected commitment-wise than there was a long time ago.
>
> It has enriched me in my job as well. You are dealing with the same situations in football, and you get the same type of scenarios in the workplace. The job is fairly stressful nowadays, so it is nice to have an outlet. I find during the off-season I will work longer because I haven't got to go to training. So things like having to go to training. Sometimes even like now I think, 'Oh god, I have to go to training tonight, how am I going to fit that in?' But it makes you have that definite break and gives you that ... I enjoy giving back something to the game because I have got a lot out of it.

A lifetime developing women's football in Victoria, since the late 1970s up until the current season, has shaped Deb's view on the game's need to succeed and how it has helped make her the woman she is today.

> Because I have been involved so long, I have seen all of the changes in Victoria, and I did a lot of work at Cranbourne to keep the profile up. Whether the Victorian Football Association has ever jumped on news about some of the veterans, they are very good with today's stars, they are brilliant. But I don't know if they have called upon some of the players that came before, that laid the foundations, to be more involved. There are a couple that are involved, Maggie Koumi and Theresa Deas who are heavily involved and I have played with Theresa. But I think a lot of players who were very, very good and did a lot for women's football have just walked away and not put anything back in. I don't really like the admin side of it. Instead, I put something back into the game through coaching, and that is where I get my enjoyment.
>
> Yeah, the good and the bad, the ups and the downs. Life's not fair, and how much effort you put into something is what you get back out of it. There are no shortcuts in anything in football. You need to put the effort into training. I was fully committed through the best team years. When some people want to go and do other things, I was boring as bat shit. I wouldn't go out and

> drink and get stupid during those years I was playing a lot of representative football. I didn't go skiing and silly things like that. I was totally dedicated to football. I think it has made me more tolerant to a certain degree. I'm getting older and less tolerant.
>
> It shows in my workplace. If you don't work hard and you are not determined ... Whatever I do, I don't do it by half—I am full on. Someone made a comment at a work conference. You had to say one thing they didn't know about you, and there were two or three managers at the conference. When it got to me, I said I had played for the Matildas, and he went, 'That explains a lot!' If I do it, I do it full on. I don't do it by half. Even if I was dealing with a customer, I would do everything I could do to make that experience for the customer in my job the best experience. I never do anything by half.

Football taught Deb that nothing is achieved without hard work, dedication and commitment. But she realises it is difficult for women who aspire to be representative players in today's professional environment.

> It is hard to get girls to sacrifice. I was fortunate when I played that the training commitment in those years when I was working wasn't as much as what it is now. You had your two nights training, maybe three. Now it's five nights a week training—commitment, commitment, commitment. I probably couldn't have done my job and played for my national team. It's hard for the girls to commit to that. At the end of the day, you have to get your education because you've got to get a job because as a female your job is going to pay your way. You are not earning 30,000 pounds a week as an English footballer.

Women's football has come far since Deb first pulled on the boots. While the women I interviewed recognised that progress, they were quick to highlight the importance of acknowledging the pioneers.

> We wear shin pads now. (Laughter.) Quality of pitches, quality of players, technically they are so much better, quality of coaches. The whole administration of women's football in Victoria was run totally by Betty Hoar, basically out of her house. And to that effect, FFV acknowledged her. We wouldn't be sitting down having this conversation because she started everything. Women's Premier League now gets a referee and two linesmen. We would have been hoping to get a referee, let alone two official linesmen. More artificial pitches, more professional, we don't all play on Sunday. That used to

be the standard—everyone would play Sunday, and rarely do we play Sunday now. Yes, it has gone from somewhere down here to somewhere up here.

Football has many different meanings to those who played it, and the women impose their own values and practices on the game and incorporate their own meanings into the part they played.

> Obviously, playing for so long over the journey there are lots of friends we have made and lifelong friends that we stay in contact with today. Up until my surgeon said you can't play anymore, I miss playing, but I have no regrets. I'm sure my body is going to tell me in 10 years' time, 'You silly bugger, you are going to suffer.' I wouldn't change anything, and that includes the highs and the lows. It's been wonderful; I could have been doing a lot of worse things.

The women clearly didn't play for the money. Breaking into a male-dominated game as a player, then coaching—which remains one of the last male-dominated bastions—speaks volumes to Deb's drive and commitment to achieve.

> If I was a bloke, I probably would have made (a) fortune. That's probably the only difference: I wouldn't be working. It's funny, from a coaching perspective, I do get some pay now, but it was very minimal five years ago and now I get paid. I don't do it for the money.
>
> If you were a male, you would get a lot more. I know what male coaches get paid. I used to know what the male coaches got paid at Casey compared to me. You don't do it for the money. For female players to make that commitment to do all that training on the possibility they might go on—where(as) I think lads have got a different scenario that they could be half as good a footballer as some of the females, that they can earn money out of the game.
>
> I can't see it in my lifetime, women earning good money out of playing football. Very few do it.

Deb continues to support young women and girls through her coaching role at Southern United.

> I put something back into the game through coaching, and that is where I get my enjoyment. I have tried to make it more professional in my time as a coach, just to make sure the women are treated equally wherever they are.

8. Heather Reid AM

It's just in my feminist nature that I wanted to make sure that women had the opportunity.

The 1980s saw the centralisation of women's football to the Australian Capital Territory (ACT). The AWSA moved their headquarters there in 1986 to develop a relationship with the Australian Sports Commission (ASC), which became strong supporters of the women's game. And with the move came greater access to government funding, which had led to the employment of the AWSA's first national executive director, Keith Gilmour, in 1985. It was during this reformation that Heather Reid entered the game. Yet though central to the heart of Australia's game, Heather's roots ran deep and from far afield.

> My parents emigrated from Edinburgh, Scotland, in 1955 and ended up in Goulburn (NSW). My maternal grandmother was there. She'd immigrated the year before and just through a range of circumstances she ended up in Goulburn. I have three siblings, two brothers and a sister, so I'm the third. My parents came here with my older brother and sister and then I was born in '56 and my other brother was born in '57.
>
> My dad got a job on the Snowy Mountains Scheme in 1957, and we spent our time travelling around the Snowy Mountains from Cooma, Khancoban and Talbingo for pretty much most of my life until I finished school in Tumut in 1973.

Scotland has a deep history as a footballing nation, even boasting the second-oldest national football association in the world—and few rivalries are better known than Celtic versus Rangers. But when I interviewed her, Heather was quick to state her heritage had little to do with how she ended up in women's football.

> My dad was a walker. He walked everywhere. Even from the time when they were in Edinburgh and when he met my mother, he would walk from one end

of Edinburgh to the other to meet her after work and then walk her home and that sort of stuff. No, he wasn't an athlete, and neither was my mother. My mother was a dancer; she liked to dance, Scottish country dancing and whatnot.

Even my brothers and my sister didn't play football, and I have six nephews and they never played football. But I have one niece who plays, so I can't really say it's my Scottish heritage that led me to play—not at all. I think it's just in my feminist nature that I wanted to make sure that women had the opportunity.

As a girl, Heather saw her first football game when she watched the men from the Snowy Mountains Hydro Electric Scheme camps play in the local league. At its peak in 1959, around 7,000 migrants were living in single quarters and barracks in Talbingo after arriving from Europe after the end of WWII. More than 100,000 men and women from 32 countries worked on the scheme over a 25-year period. Witnessing first-hand how the many different cultures combined on and off the pitch introduced Heather to the multicultural element of football, not knowing then how much of a role it would play in her future working life.

Growing up in the Snowy Mountains was when I first saw soccer played, you know, when it was men from the barracks, you know, I went down onto the local oval and they were playing soccer, and I kicked the ball around with some friends when I was about 15 or 16. That was also when I first understood the cultural differences because the Croatians were on one team and the Serbians were on another. (Laughter.) So it's throughout my career, there's been this interwoven sort of multicultural aspect as well as diversity and family and inclusion and all that sort of stuff as well. That's what I value about the sport.

Heather spent her childhood and youth in the Snowy Mountains region working locally and enjoying the outdoor life and travelled by bus to school in Tumut. After finishing school in 1973, she moved to the national capital to further her studies.

When I finished school, I came to Canberra to do a secretarial course. I then worked as a typist and secretary for a year and then I travelled overseas. When I got back from overseas, I was working at the Australian National University (ANU) as a secretary and there was a group of women who were playing soccer in a lunchtime competition. This was in 1977.

The women playing were looking for others at the university who might be interested in forming a club and to get a women's competition going on the weekends. A work colleague introduced Heather to the game in 1977, and while playing for the ANU in 1978, she helped to form the ANU Women's Soccer Club. In 1979, Heather worked with the other women to form the ACT Women's Soccer Association (ACTWSA) and was the first Grounds and Fixtures Officer. While the men's association (ACT Soccer Federation) generally accepted the women, it was in reality only toleration, and the women knew they could do a better job on their own.

> I was one of the people who helped start a new women's club, and we played in a 10-team competition under the jurisdiction of what was then the ACT Soccer Federation's Junior Committee. In 1978, we convened a meeting and decided to form the ACT Women's Soccer Association, mainly because we felt that we could do a better job at organising the league and grounds and fixtures and all (that) sort of stuff. We then had our own association, and we wanted to be part of the AWSA at the time and play in national championships and all those other wonderful things that were available.
>
> I was selected in the first ACT representative squad, and this stage, you know, I'm 22, 23 years of age so I didn't actually start playing until I was 22. Then we had the first ACT rep team that I was selected for, but I withdrew for different reasons, and the team went to play in Adelaide in our first national championship.

That was in 1980, and Heather went as the manager of the ACT team.

From those early days, Heather's administrative career in football exploded, and she was soon juggling several positions with the ACTWSA, including secretary, vice president and president. And in 1983, she was the first coach of the ACT U/15 team.

> I was the first Grounds and Fixtures Officer for ACT Women's Soccer, and then I got involved at the national level. So I stayed involved with ACT as secretary and vice president and president. I was also, you know, maintaining my playing commitments throughout, but also a coach and a team manager, and then I got involved with the Australian Women's Association as a member on the Board. I was wearing two or three hats, you know, being on the committee of ACT Women's Soccer, being a player. I coached the ACT under-15s team one year and I coached the under-17s.

With her administrative jobs mounting, Heather enrolled in Sports Management at the Canberra College of Advanced Education (now the University of Canberra) in 1981, graduating in 1983.

> From then, after a year of working with ACT Touch Football, I ended up working for Australian Women's Soccer as their National Executive Officer for about seven years.

As an executive member of the ACTWSA, Heather attended each of the national championships after ACT's inclusion in the AWSA in 1980. Heather also volunteered as team manager for the national women's team on several occasions, including the national tour to Taiwan in 1984, and travelled with the team as tour leader for international tours to Dallas in 1987 and as executive director on the tour to China in 1988.

> You know, I was only 28 at that time, sounds a bit crazy, doesn't it? But I wasn't that much older than a lot of the players in fact.

After a redraft of the AWSA constitution in 1985, the executive became a Board with a president, vice president and five new directors. Heather was elected as Director of Promotions and Marketing and now worked alongside both Elaine Watson and Betty Hoar (among others) in the drive to improve opportunities for women playing football on a domestic and international level.

During that same year, the AWSA submitted a grant application to the Australian Sports Commission (ASC) for funding to help employ a National Executive Director (NED). The application succeeded, and the AWSA received $25,000 with which it appointed Keith Gilmour in April 1985. Gilmour resigned seven months later, and in February 1986 Heather replaced him as the second AWSA NED and moved the headquarters to Canberra.

During this period, Heather learned of the need to develop contacts within the Oceania and Asia regions, and was part of a small group canvassing FIFA for a world cup for women.

> Then in '86, I was appointed as NED, and so in that capacity, I was working full time in the sport and travelled with the national team mostly as the tour leader, and we had managers like Elaine Watson and Betty Hoar and Stephanie Quinn—you know, the pioneers of the of the administration of the

sport, really they were. We were still battling with FIFA to get a Women's World Cup and get Olympic status and things like that.

The group was successful. The first FIFA Women's World Cup was held in China in 1991, and as the NED of AWSA, Heather attended the historic event as a media representative because the national team had failed to qualify through the Oceania confederation.

Heather had finally found her dream job: being paid for bringing more opportunities to women in football. But times were different then, and Heather recalls the humble beginnings of life in the new AWSA office.

It was pretty interesting because it was just me and a typewriter in an office at Sports House in Hackett. Eventually I got a part-time assistant, and then I think we ended up with a computer as well and a fax machine, but very sort of primitive administrative tools compared to where we're at today with email and mobile phones and all that sort of stuff.

In 1990, while NED, Heather was invited to attend the ninth Dana Cup in Denmark as an observer. Heralded as one of the world's largest youth football tournaments, the cup has been held annually since 1982. Elaine Watson explains this trip provided the AWSA with valuable first-hand experience managing large events and, through Heather's contacts, provided opportunities for two Australians, Carol Vinson and Julie Murray, to sign playing contracts with the host Danish Club Fortuna Hjorring. This spotlighted the beginning of Australian women players gaining access to international football leagues and professional clubs—now the norm in the 2020 game.

Heather stayed with the AWSA until 1992, but returned to the game in the late 1990s heading into the Sydney 2000 Olympic Games.

I was on the Board at the time when the Matildas or the national team wanted to do the calendar.

That was the Matildas' nude calendar of 1999. The players were fighting for recognition and resources in the lead-up to the Sydney Olympics, and opted to pose nude to draw attention. Its publication under the title, *The Matildas: the new fashion in football*, grabbed the attention of many. It was controversial and garnered media attention, but it did little to raise much-needed funds for the women involved.

After Heather left the AWSA, the association came under pressure to amalgamate with the ASF. AWSA members were conflicted between maintaining a single focus on the development of the women's game and the potential benefits for future development under the ASF's authority.

Due to widespread and ongoing mismanagement in the game, the federal government appointed businessman David Crawford to undertake a review of the game management and governance of the game in 2001. Commonly referred to as the 'Crawford Report' and completed in 2002, it secured wide support from the football community and spectators.

Amongst the 53 recommendations was one that existing state and territory federations amalgamate with the ASF.

The recommendations intended to benefit women's football and help it grow with fairer and more equitable treatment and better wages, coaching and security, but many misgivings remained. In reality, the report's reforms only underlined football authorities' lack of understanding about the women's game and, rather than resolve the challenges women's football faced, left the players no better off.

In the wake of the Crawford Report, FFA eventually replaced the ASF, and the A-League was instituted in 2005. As the men's game was being shaken up, so the women's faced upheaval. Heather was convinced to rejoin the world of football management that year when she was headhunted for a controversial new role.

> I was tapped on the shoulder to apply to be the CEO of Soccer Canberra, knowing that the integration of four organisations here needed to take place given the Crawford recommendations and everything else and some government push to make that happen.
>
> One of my first tasks was to do a management review and restructure of Soccer Canberra. We had five staff, we were almost insolvent, there was no money in the bank, but we got some government support to help us go through the integration process, which took probably three or four years.

Heather was the first woman to be appointed as a CEO of a state-based federation. However, according to some of her friends in the women's association, she had gone over to the dark side and was now working for the enemy. They resented the forced closure of some organisations and resultant restructure. Ultimately, Women's Soccer Canberra folded and handed its affairs over to Soccer Canberra, which was then rebranded as Capital Football in 2005 under a new model constitution.

> I didn't want it to become part of that old soccer. It was rebranded so we were all part of ACT Football Federation trading as Capital Football, so it's all now one integrated organisation. I've got 16 staff and a budget of $3 million so it works, and the women are doing extremely well.

After the A-League was launched, FFA moved their attention to the formation of the W-League. Canberra Eclipse had previously represented the national capital in the former National Women's Soccer League, but when the FFA initiated the new W-League in 2008 their place within it was uncertain.

> When they first sort of floated the W-League and they said it's going to be based on the A-League model, meaning that the A-League clubs would have to support women's teams. That was a bit of a kick in the guts for me because I thought, well, we don't have an A-League team.
>
> We had a high number of players in the national team, and we had a Board that was committed to supporting women's football as part of our player pathway and also part of our overall game development strategy. So I had to go and negotiate, cajole and convince FFA that Canberra should have a team in the W-League.

While Heather was pleased she secured Canberra's inclusion, she is outspoken about the W-League model. She believes that the current format is unsuitable for the women's game and believes there should be a complete home and away series.

Heather resigned from Capital Football after 12 years in 2016. During these years, she led the development of women's football, but the journey has not always been an easy one. Being a woman in a male-dominated sporting organisation often presented challenges: she fought ingrained sexism from day one.

Those threatened by women in power targeted Heather viciously. She has faced sexist, homophobic and abusive comments and bullying on social media. Over the years, detractors have called her incompetent, fraudulent, racist and gender-biased for promoting and developing women's football.

> I've had people in the early years who were a bit sceptical. Blokes were sceptical about a woman being able to do this job. I've had challenges where some Board members have accused me of misleading the Board or not being loyal to the Board just because of lack of information or untimely release of information or whatever. And sometimes, I think the way I've been treated at

Board level, I would question whether or not a man would have been treated the same.

Heather says her biggest challenge as CEO is people seeing her deliver a message and attacking her personally rather than her position.

> What I do in my job is not necessarily what Heather Reid would like to do, but it's what I have to do as CEO. And also understanding that Capital Football, for example, is more than just Heather Reid, and it's an organisation, it's the clubs, it's the players, it's everybody that's involved. But sometimes when the finger gets pointed at Capital Football, as an example, it's actually being pointed at me, which becomes personal. And I've had my share of people standing in my face and abusing me and calling me nasty names, particularly in Croatia a few years ago. It was a pretty horrible experience that I went through.
>
> I still have to, you know, carry out that direction. I think that's been the biggest challenge across a range of issues and even going right back to the whole integration and amalgamation. The tension or the struggle sometimes between the personal versus the professional or the personal and the political, the personal and the business objectives. There are things that I have to do in my job that I don't like doing, they're not things that I personally would want to do.
>
> Delivering messages to clubs that they're no longer in the Premier League, you know, delivering messages that you know a key club official is going to be suspended for a year because of his bad behaviour. I'm the messenger, and sometimes those messages aren't very nice to deliver, but I still have to do them. So then I become the bitch, then I become that 'HEATHER REID CAPITAL FOOTBALL' and that can be pretty difficult to deal with sometimes.

Heather's commitment to the game has seen her win numerous awards. These include life memberships with the ACTWSA in 1986, Womensport and Recreation ACT in 1998 and the ACT Football Federation in 2004. She also won the Australian Sports Medal in 2001 and the Australian Sports Commission's Margaret Pewtress Memorial Award in 2006. The highlights of these acknowledgements were being inducted in to the FFA Hall of Fame in 2007 and being awarded a Member of the Order of Australia for her contribution to the sport in 2015. Heather then revisited the University of Canberra in 2017 to receive an Honorary Doctorate for her distinguished service to sport administration, football and as an advocate for gender equality.

Looking back on her career, Heather pinpoints the support of her family as key to her success and reflects on the rise of women's football in recent years.

> I've got total support from my family; that's critical for me to be able to do what I do. You know, my parents were probably a little bit surprised in the early days—like many people, including others involved in football and the media. Women's participation was seen as a novelty, you know. We were causing trouble because we wanted access to grounds and referees and money and international competition and things like that. So we were rocking the boat somewhat, you know, but I've always seen my involvement as one that's about wanting equity for everyone involved in the game and having, you know, similar rights and opportunities to the game as men and boys have.
>
> It's a fantastic game for women and girls to be able to be involved in as players, administrators. I'd love to see more leaders, love to see more coaches, you know. It's the true world sport that anybody should be able to participate in and that's what I've been striving to get recognised for the last 30-odd years. So my family and my friends very much support that, and I think over the 30-odd years we've seen a significant shift in the attitude of the old guard that was involved. Some of them are still there but women's participation is no longer a novelty, it's no longer something that is tolerated. It's embraced, and it's even encapsulated in Sepp Blatter's comments that 'the future of football is feminine'. But across the board, football is one of the few sports that women, families can enjoy together, so I think that's really important, and I've got nothing but total support from my family for what I've been able to do.

Heather was elected to the FFA Board in 2018 and was voted off the Board in 2021. She published a book in 2020 with Dr Marion Stell titled, *Women in Boots: Football and Feminism in the 1970s*.

9. Carolyn Monk

A lot of people that I've met have become lifelong friends. That's probably the most memorable.

After a comparatively late start to the game at the age of 17, Carolyn Monk was soon to rise to the top of the women's game in Australia. Not long after she began her playing career with Watsonia Heights Soccer Club in 1980, Carolyn was selected to play for Victoria at the national championships in the same year. After many strong performances in the eight championships she attended, leading to her winning the McQuarrie-Rocco award for the most valuable state player, Carolyn went on to play for Australia in 1989.

The Watsonia Heights Football Club is celebrating its 50th anniversary in 2021, including the development of the women's game within the club. Carolyn Monk is to be recognised as the only female player to reach national team selection.

When I first met Carolyn Monk in 2012, she was still playing football with the Darebin Falcons at the age of 49. A pioneer recognised for her contribution to the Victoria state team and the Matildas, Carolyn was born in Melbourne in 1963 and started playing with local team Watsonia Heights Soccer Club (WHSC) in 1980. She was 17—a comparatively late start considering some players in the Victorian women's competition were just 12. It was the first year that WHSC had fielded a women's team, and they joined 15 other women's teams playing in the metropolitan area that year. With Carolyn's help, they reached the semi-finals in the second division competition.

WHSC is the same club that football pioneers Betty and Mick Hoar had helped to set up during the previous decade. Betty Hoar was at the club when she was appointed to the role of secretary of the VWSA in 1984 and as the vice president in 1985. Carolyn came to soccer because, as she puts it, 'I was kicked out of class.' And soccer was not even her first choice.

> When I was younger, I just wanted to play AFL, but there was no scope to play at all. I couldn't even play in a boys' team. Someone said, 'Come and

> play soccer,' and I said, 'Well, it depends, because if it's on Saturday I've got to the football (AFL) so there's no way I'm going to play soccer.' I was very AFL-minded as a child. I eventually went down the following year. I think I made the state team in the first or second year. Betty's husband was coaching; that might have had something to do with it.

Family support helped Carolyn play football, but her employer placed restrictions on her that made it very difficult for her to continue playing, majorly impacting her state representative career. Financial support for women to play sport was virtually non-existent in the 1980s.

> My family were relatively supportive. At work, it was hard to get time off a lot of the time because it wasn't recognised. I'm sure if I were male, I would have been given some status, but not as a female. Probably for about five years, I didn't play for the state team because I couldn't get the time off. I eventually left that job and made the state team. However, most employers were reluctant to approve leave, whether paid or unpaid.

Despite these obstacles, Carolyn went on to play for the Victorian state team in eight national championships beginning in 1980. Like many other women players at that time, they often decided to change clubs if they felt unsupported or were chasing higher levels of competition. Sometimes, the women just got sick and tired of being discriminated against.

> I got to meet all these other people and I thought, 'Oh wow, there's so much more to this game.' And the following year, I went to Greensborough, which was the best team in the competition. They used to win everything and there was only one other team worth playing, which was Dandenong at the time. Greensborough used to win like 12:0 against every team and still beat Dandenong, but it was only by a couple of goals. (Greensborough was successful in the early years, but Dandenong did win a lot of silverware in the coming years.) Then from Greensborough, we moved the whole team to Coburg. We played at Coburg for a couple of years but got jack of having to pay the way for the men. We had to fundraise for the men to play, and they were in fourth division, which just wasn't right considering the women's team had four national players including myself. We ended up packing up and moving to Nunawading.

It was at the Nunawading club that Carolyn met Nicky Leitch, and they quickly became good friends. They then both chose to move again to the South Melbourne Hellas club in 1992, which had first introduced women's teams in 1979. While women were beginning to break down some of the barriers that prevented them from playing the game, many male-dominated clubs refused to recognise them. This lack of acknowledgment resulted in the women pioneers' experiences being excluded from the wider history of the game. This is evident in the history of the game at the South Melbourne club, where there is little indication that a women's team existed at all.

> The disappointing thing for me with South Melbourne is that we were the pioneers of the women's team, but there's no recognition, history or anything.

During her time with the Victorian state team, Carolyn was awarded the McQuarrie-Rocco award for the most valuable Victorian state team player in 1989. The award was initiated to memorialise two outstanding young women players who tragically lost their lives in a car accident while returning from a game in Sydney. Carolyn also received a bronze award from the AWSA in 1990 for playing in seven or more national championships for Victoria.

In 1989, the Japanese Football Association (JFA) invited Australia to compete in a combined test and provincial tour of Japan. On December 4 of that year, Carolyn was selected to play for the women's national team where she played three games against Japan, Prima Kunoichi and Yomiuri. Australia went undefeated.

> Making the Australian team in 1989, which I never thought I would, is probably my most memorable moment considering I started playing at such a late age. Going to Japan with the Matildas was incredible, but the lifelong friends I've made from football has been truly amazing.

While Carolyn is not involved with the game anymore, she has remained in contact with the many friends she has made throughout her career.

> I retired at about 28 and went back at 38 and played for another year or two and retired again and started playing again at 47. I'm not involved with the game really, but I'm still involved with friends that I've made. Friends just are the best thing.

10. Maggie Koumi

It's not a men's game anymore.

Maggie Koumi is one of the longest-serving pioneers of the women's game in Victoria. She came to it in 1981 at 29 and has spent close to 40 years as both a player and an administrator. Maggie played a key role in assisting the women's game negotiate the many obstacles faced during the amalgamation of the VWSA and the VSF in the late 1990s.

Women's football at that point needed an advocate to stand up for the survival and development of women's football while at the same time preserve the history of the game. Maggie Koumi always made herself available to do the work required to support women's football. She is still involved today as a member of the FV Historical Committee.

When I interviewed her, Maggie was living in the northern suburbs of Melbourne, but she was born in the rugby town of Twickenham in England in 1950.

> I came here for a holiday in 1977 and then decided I wanted to come back for a bit longer, so I went home and got a new visa and came back in 1979 for a 12-month holiday, and I am still here!

Like a lot of immigrants Maggie, who had always played sport, sought out familiar faces, which eventually led her to a local football team.

> I knew a lot of other English people and they basically—a lot of the women were playing in a social team—and the minute they saw another pom, that was it. You were told to get a pair of boots, you had to join the team. That's how I got involved. I had never played in my life before that. I never really followed the game in England, and I lived around the corner from Stanford Bridge for a long time. I wasn't interested. I used to play netball. I wasn't aware that women played football back then in England. I never heard of it.

> My brother's stepfamily are all big football players, one of them was playing for Stoke City. He is doing very well, and a couple of others are doing very well.

Maggie's parents supported her interest in sport generally but had a poor awareness of women's football. Her father, like many male football supporters, trivialised women's participation based on their perception of the general lack of skill.

> Mum and Dad have always known I was a sporty person, but they hadn't heard of football either as far as females playing. When they came over for a holiday, they came and had a look at my game. Dad didn't think much of it, of course—very amateurish-type playing. Blokes didn't understand social football.

The support of friends and community, however, was a big influence on her and other women's long-term involvement in the game. Friendship and the enjoyment of playing often overrode the need to win.

> A lot of my friends were playing, and other friends got involved on the social side because there was always some type of social event going on. My whole life revolved around the game. It started to become a major central focus for everything. Friends and family were either playing football or part of the social group. A lot of people played sport in summer, cricket or whatever, so the group got bigger and bigger as everybody started to share grounds and rooms. The social side got bigger and bigger as you interacted with the clubs that you went to.

Maggie began playing in 1981 when she joined an all-women's team.

> The first team I played for was called All Suburbs because we were from all over the place. We didn't really have a home, and it was just a team that tried to latch on to different clubs to lend us their grounds and changing rooms.

The Victorian State League had been split into two divisions in 1974 and remained that way until 1984. Maggie played with a number of clubs representing both divisions during her 20 years as a player.

> All Suburbs fell apart and then reformed as Melbourne Suburbs but didn't last very long, just a transient team. I then played with Melbourne University for

> about nine years. I did coaching as well as playing and then got drafted onto the committees and got more involved in the committee side as well. Then I went over to Darebin Falcons, a big women's sports club. I was there for a couple of years as they were trying to establish themselves in soccer. They had a big women's football team over there. I went over to Box Hill for a year. I was then told to pack up the boots.
>
> They weren't Premier League clubs. I played for Divisions 2 and 3. When I first started, there were only two divisions. A very low level. I wasn't very good—just a social player.

Like many of the other women involved in football during these formative years, Maggie only stayed with clubs that supported her. This was particularly true of ethnic-based clubs, which either barred women from playing or trivialised those who did. Historically, women participated in the off-field roles associated with the social aspects of clubs.

> We didn't interact with the male side of things, especially my side of town, which was the Northern Suburbs, which were very ethnic clubs. And women weren't really part of the playing aspect, unless you were in the canteen, which was pretty much it. We didn't have a lot to do with clubs like that. We weren't really welcomed. Nobody took women's football seriously back then, apart from other women and other female players.

Migrant women largely did not play football; however, they were crucial to the continued existence of many clubs because of their input into the social side of the game and the work they undertook in the many behind-the-scenes roles.

> I think it was because of the ethnicity and in general a lot of people, men, thought women shouldn't play football. They would look at it and see the standard and they would berate it. The standard was not really relevant. It was either you are playing or you're not playing.
>
> Most of us didn't bother going near a lot of the clubs, simply because you knew their attitude. If you knew there was a problem in an area, you just didn't go anywhere near it. It was a lost cause as far as we were concerned. We were pretty powerless with having any inroads to clubs like that. This is from a social point of view. There was a lot of resentment. A lot of clubs, I think, once they found the girls hit around 13 they shouldn't be playing. Basically,

if they were wearing a bra, they shouldn't be playing. It is okay for female children to play. That was sort of an attitude around those ethnic-based clubs. As long as the women supported that, too, and the mums would agree with it, you had no choice really, or any way to help them transition into women's teams.

The ones that were strong ethnic clubs were the Greek and Italian predominantly or your variance through all that. They were strongholds within their own club. Players from other backgrounds weren't always welcomed as well, not only females I think. Once that attitude started to water down, people realised there is a bit more about football, then it changed, and women started to make inroads within clubs. And then (the) Women's Premier League became part of the Federation and then our game was played before the men's Premier League grand final and people accepted it more.

In 2000, Maggie was asked to apply for manager of the Senior Women's State Team. The National Training Centre Program was the elite program at the time. As she spent time with the state squad, Maggie began to see changes in how women were treated. At first, attitudes were hard to budge, especially if the women's team made a habit of defeating the boys.

We would go into clubs, and if the girls beat the boys, we often found there was a lot of resentment there. That was always an interesting scenario. I remember one club, the parents, mums, coming up to us and abusing us for letting the girls beat the boys. We shouldn't have allowed it. We should have let the boys win. The boy's Super League is under-14s, so about the same size. That kind of attitude was around a little bit.

However, once the male-dominated clubs started to realise that the girls could play well, they slowly began to accept them. This was an experience common to many women and girls during these developing years.

People were actually able to see women play football. A lot of clubs had never ever seen a female play, and that really was the catalyst of changing the way some clubs thought and women themselves within a club. Mums would get in there and try to get something done other than working in the canteen. (Laughter.) It was part of everything, there was a bit of everything that helped spark it all off and made it shift. But again, all that changed very quickly; once one club started it, and you start to make inroads in others, you get accepted quite quickly. Within a club itself, of course, as the committees change and the younger ones come in, it is a different attitude of people.

We slowly found, just over that short period, say 2002 to 2006, more and more clubs were happy to have the girls play against them. They recognised the skill because it was an elite squad. They recognised these girls could actually play and they didn't mind. They were quite happy to support it. So in a short space of time, it started to grow (in) acceptance quite quickly.

For example, (with the) women playing first division, other people saw that women could actually play the game. It became more and more accepted in some clubs. Some clubs embraced a team and supported them. Some clubs even looked after the women better than the men, which was good, because the women's team was more successful. A lot of it was based on skill and success rather than the fact that females were players. It was an interesting turn around (of) mindset with some clubs.

Maggie's skills as an administrator grew over the many years of her involvement, beginning with her role as social secretary with the All Suburbs team. 'We took it in turns to attend the club meetings, when each club had to meet with the Federation.'

This new role allowed to her better assist women navigate the many challenges that the amalgamation of the VWSA and the VSF would present. Historian Ted Simmons states that during 1997 and 1978, the two organisations were still discussing the possibility of an amalgamation. The women's association had become too much for a volunteer committee to continue to manage as player numbers continued to grow. The president of the association at the time, Peter Athanasiadis, took the proposal of amalgamation to the AGM in 1998. After much discussion, the motion was passed. To ensure an equitable move for the women, the association stated that a women's management committee be set up with the chair of that committee sitting on the new VSF Board.

> The women's association was independent of the men's back then, that (amalgamation) didn't happen until 1999. In about 1997/98, I was on the Board of Directors of Women's Soccer in Victoria. When the men and women came together, the federation invited people from the Board of Women's Soccer Victoria to form the women's committee with Football Federation Victoria. I was on that committee.

Women's football had now entered a new era under the jurisdiction of the VSF. Consequently, all competitions, state teams and programs were run according to the VSF constitution and the amalgamation agreement. Maggie's friend Theresa Deas (Jones) worked in conjunction with the new members as an advisor and negotiator to provide continuity and information regarding current development and state programs run by AWSA.

In 1999 Women's Soccer Victoria (WSV) and the VSF amalgamated. A new structure was established to provide more professional services and infrastructure for the future development of the women's game.

> In 2001, I was headhunted—asked to come and meet the Board and after about six months I was then invited to join the Board. I was there for about six years. I had to hang up the boots. I was allowed to play in the World Masters Games but that was it. I had to be independent. No more playing. I was 51 when I hung up my boots. I started late and finished late.
>
> I played all up probably a bit less than 20 years. I kept playing for a long time. I was old and grey. I got onto the federation Board of Directors, and the Board didn't allow us to be involved with any club; you had to be independent, so I had to stop playing. That was in 2001.

While the VSF was structured to support the development of women's football after the years of progress achieved by the VWSA, changes to the hierarchy of management reflecting this new direction were a long time coming.

> At the Board level, I found the biggest hurdles. Back then it was simply they had no choice. They had to put a female from women's football on the Board. We were given a little bit of lip service. I didn't believe that they took it seriously. Most of the Board at that time didn't give a damn about it. It was very much pissing in the wind. I tended to deal with stuff directly because back then each member had a portfolio, and mine was women's football. We did a lot of interaction with staff, and I basically worked with the staff as much as I could without having to worry about the board.

In 2006, a new constitution was developed for the VSF. Up until that point, the men's Premier League and the men's state body essentially ran the sport—'nobody else got a say,' explains Maggie. When the new constitution was implemented in 2007, the then FFV board was dissolved, and Maggie and the rest of the Board members stood down to make way for the new voting system. The new constitution provided an opportunity for the clubs to be more involved in the running of the federation and in particular provided an avenue for more women to be involved in leadership roles.

> The new constitution was formed, with some of us pushing for it and some of us not. There was an election, and all clubs had the right to vote for zone reps, then those zone reps voted for a new Board.
> Everybody had a chance to vote. No women got voted on. So we ended up with no women on the Board, which was a bit of a shame. That hasn't been an issue since then because they have co-opted other women on. There were two of us on the Board when we had to dissolve for the new constitution, but no women got voted on at the new elections, so they co-opted two to three women on then. At the last elections, it was the first time a woman got voted onto the Board of Directors. They had in the past always been co-opted, never been voted on. That was a good move forward, that was progress. So it has been a long time coming (20 years) before a woman got voted onto the board.
> When I was on the board, I got to meet all the presidents of the men's Premier League Clubs. They were very receptive to me. Initially, they didn't want to know, but once they got to know my face and saw me around and realised I wasn't scary, they were very good, they were very polite. I found it was quite good, as far as the administration level goes. It's a little bit different when you try and push the women's teams and get something for them within the club. I had to leave it to the women themselves within their own club to do that. With a new constitution, everyone has a right to vote so really it was up to people themselves to change their own clubs. We gave them the tools to do it; we couldn't do it for them.

So women were finding their voice, but they still lacked money. This, however, was never the case for the men.

> The men used to have an annual trip to China, partly sponsored by the Chinese and partly funded by the federation. We took the women's elite squad to China, and we had to pay for ourselves. The board gave us $3000 for a physio to take with us—where they had been going for the last 10 years, given $20,000 every year to take a representative men's squad. They pick

> three players from each Premier League team, and half the board would go off to China for a couple of weeks, all expenses paid.
>
> So, there was a big difference back then. That kind of thing was very much brought to a head and stopped in the end. Really, just making a noise about it made it stop. That was very much the old-school board. Nobody would ever consider that now. All those people have gone.

As there were no women elected to the new Board, Maggie took a couple of years away from football after her tenure on the VSF board ended.

> I knew the women's committee were looking for new people, so I put my hand up and stood for election and got into it. I was then elected the chairperson for that committee. I have been there the last two years. Every two years you have to re-stand. It would be three years now. We are advisory to the board on women's matters. The women's committee is anything to do with women's football. I am also on the junior committee, which is boys' and girls' football, which is a big link as far as women and girls go. A lot of junior girls play in the women's leagues, so there is a big connection as far as female football goes.

Maggie is still involved today and currently sits on the FFV Historical Committee. Tony Dunkerley, president of FFV, formed the committee in December 2008, with Maggie as an inaugural member.

> I am still involved on the historical committee, which has been going for a couple of years now. People don't want to see the history lost. We advise the board with things like the Victorian Hall of Fame, which we didn't have before. It was good to get that up. We sourced candidates for that, and we now also overview the applications for life memberships. All under Board approval of course. At least it gives us a link, which is firm and useful to everybody.
>
> The other thing that has really happened through the junior area is in schools, of course. It took the schools years to accept football for females, many years. That has helped immensely with getting football for females into (the) mainstream. But getting them to come to clubs from school is the next stage. There is a lot of dropout between school and club level. We are still working on that and hoping the federation will do a bit more work on it. There is a big gap.

Maggie still stays in touch with the many friends she made and maintains a strong link with the Board of women's football in Victoria.

> I am always fighting for the female cause, so to speak. There is always more work to be done. I question people all the time about if there is anything that is a problem or an issue that needs to be addressed. I will address it through the committee, the women's committee if it needs to go the Board. I often meet with members of the Board at different functions, and I get to meet with the Board a couple times a year anyway, so then I can get into their faces—let them know if there are any issues. They are very supportive these days.

This fighting spirit was required in the first years of the W-League, when Melbourne Victory entered the competition in 2008.

> When the W-League was created and Melbourne Victory first formed, there were virtually no Victorian players selected for the team. When I questioned this, I was told there were no Vic players up to that standard. This caused a lot of angst to me and many others, so I set upon a task of meeting with everyone I could think of to change their way of thinking. I met with the coach and other staff and basically nagged everyone up to and including the president and Board members to at least give some of the more prominent Victorian women players a chance. They listened, and eventually these Vic players were acknowledged and brought into the squad and the team. Thankfully, we have far more prominence now.
>
> It made me aware that anybody can get involved at any level. I was a crap player but I was still travelling around the country in an elite squad, meeting with top players.

Elaine Watson

Betty Hoar playing with Watsonia women's team in Melbourne, 1980

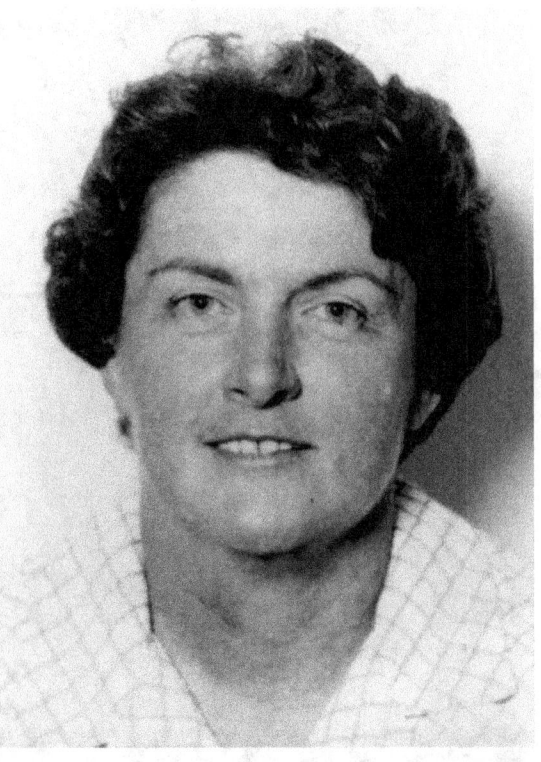

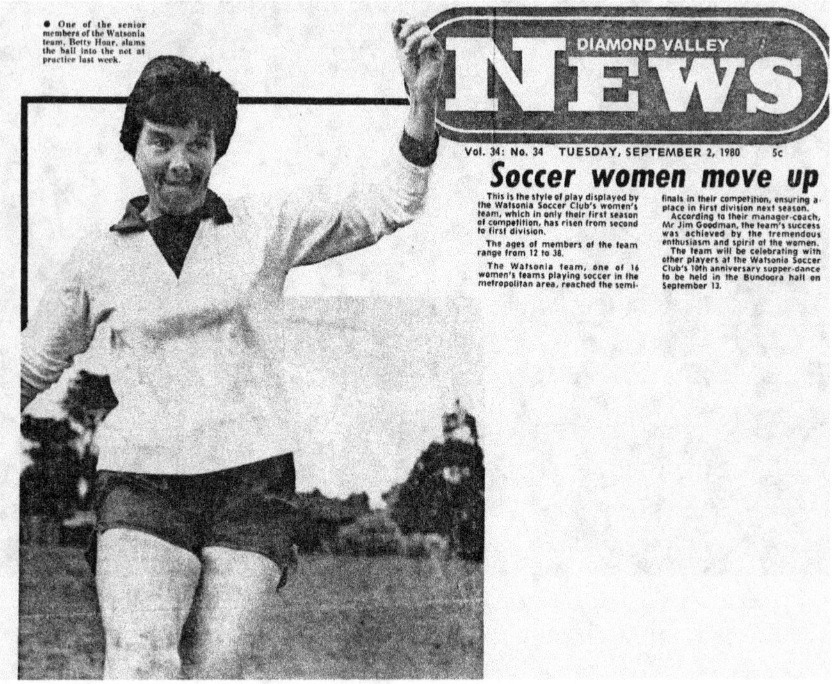

● One of the senior members of the Watsonia team, Betty Hoar, slams the ball into the net at practice last week.

DIAMOND VALLEY NEWS

Vol. 34: No. 34 TUESDAY, SEPTEMBER 2, 1980 5c

Soccer women move up

This is the style of play displayed by the Watsonia Soccer Club's women's team, which in only their first season of competition, has risen from second to first division.

The ages of members of the team range from 12 to 38.

The Watsonia team, one of 16 women's teams playing soccer in the metropolitan area, reached the semi-finals in their competition, ensuring a place in first division next season.

According to their manager-coach, Mr Jim Goodman, the team's success was achieved by the tremendous enthusiasm and spirit of the women.

The team will be celebrating with other players at the Watsonia Soccer Club's 10th anniversary supper-dance to be held in the Bundoora hall on September 13.

Three legends of the game: Betty and Mick Hoar with Rale Rasić, Melbourne, 2020

Paul Turner and Theresa Deas, Melbourne, 2020

Vicki Bugden presenting a fundraising cheque to the Salvation Army's Red Shield Appeal on behalf of Lismore Richmond Rovers FC in 2015

Deborah Nichols in her first team—Sambourne Church of England Primary School, Warminster, Wiltshire, England, 1973

Heather Reid speaking at a women's football conference at the Women's World Cup in Canada, 2015

SECOND ROW: Jane Oakley (Head Coach), Lucy Kapusta, Caroline Saville, Caroline McEvoy, Jenni Black, Nino La Scala (Physiotherapist Diane Jansen, Melissa Lovie, Leah Terek, Rachel Lamb, Maggie Koumi (Team Manager).
FRONT: Natalie Kalow, Anthea Vardakas, Jessica Humble, Chiara Romano, Alena Kapusta, Sarah Groenewald, Selin Kuralay, Melissa Ba

The Victoria Vision side in the former Women's National Soccer League, 2000.
Maggie Koumi was team manager and is in the backrow, far right.

Sharon Young with the Wentworth Waratahs women's team, 1982

Lisa Casagrande in action for the Matildas vs China, 1995

Belinda Wilson in 2019, when appointed Head Coach of Byron Bay FC

Nicky Leitch in action for South Melbourne, 1992

Louisa Bisby (centre) with Emma Rae and Melissa Barbieri in 1995.

Annette Hughes with South Melbourne women's team in 1998

Caitlin Downes playing with Byron Bay senior women's team, 2004—daughter of author Greg Downes and the reason for his involvement and interest in women's football in the first place

Jane Natoli Manager of Melbourne Victory women's W League team, 2013

11. Sharon Young

I'd never seen my dad cry, and he ran down to the fence, and he gave me the biggest hug he's ever given me and just handed me the Australian flag, and we ran across the field and it was just, yeah, I will never, ever forget that.

Sharon Young played her first game for Australia in the qualifying tournament for a chance to compete in the inaugural Women's World Cup, which was to be held in China in 1991. The series resulted in a loss for Australia and has remained a landmark result in the history of Australia's international competition as the only Women's World Cup Australia has failed to attend.

The result had a major impact on the development of women's football in Australia as well as impacting the personal contributions that the players had struggled with to reach that point in their careers. Sharon Young was one of those players.

The 1970s saw women turn their eye to the international game. Alongside football associations worldwide, AWSA began fighting FIFA for a standalone Women's World Cup. FIFA had been sponsoring world cup competitions for the men's game since 1930, and the women's associations argued FIFA should recognise their game equally. There were several false starts, with the AWSA receiving notification that the inaugural Women's World Cup would be held in Hong Kong in July 1976. Although the national competition was rescheduled and a team and management-staff selected, the World Cup announcement proved unfounded.

It was another 12 years until FIFA reluctantly came on board and announced a 'pilot' tournament. The organisation was uncertain about using their 'World Cup' brand for a women's tournament so instead named the trial event the FIFA Women's Invitational Tournament. Held in Guangdong China in 1988, Australia competed along with 11 other nations and achieved a rousing victory over Brazil in its opening match. Overall, the tournament was heralded as a great success, with 65,000 spectators attending the final game, and so FIFA announced it would sponsor the first official Women's World Cup in China in 1991. Yet still reluctant to give the tournament a full World Cup billing, FIFA named it the First FIFA World Championship for Women's Football for the M&M's Cup—after the tournament's only sponsor, Mars, Incorporated. FIFA also decided the games would last only 80 minutes because it believed women lacked the stamina to play a full 90.

Australia was part of the Oceania Football Confederation (OFC) in 1991, which was only allocated one representative spot for entry into the World Cup. Australia would have to compete with the other OFC member nations for the honour of attending the inaugural competition. As a lead-up to the World Cup qualifying tournament, Australia hosted a three-match series against the Swedish champions Malmo. They won the first but lost the last two. Then came the qualifying tournament for Oceania's lone representative, held at Club Marconi in Sydney, with competing teams Australia, New Zealand and Papua New Guinea (PNG). It was in the opening game of this series that Sharon Young played her first game for Australia.

Sharon was born in the Sydney suburb of Liverpool in 1965 and began her journey in women's football with the Wentworthville Waratahs at sixteen.

> I was playing softball for Wenty Waratahs, and I always liked soccer when I was younger because of my twin brother. I used to play in his team because they never had any girls' teams. I used to play in his team as one of the boys because I had short hair, and then I got too old to play in that team, so I played softball. One day a guy came up to me and said he was starting up a female soccer team. That was when I was 16, and that's when I started. I played with the boys for about two years and then started netball and softball, and when I was 16, I started women's soccer.

Due to the lack of financial support for women in football, Sharon relied on the full support of her family and fundraising to keep her playing.

> My family were very supportive because there's no money in any of the codes, outdoor or indoor, and everything was sponsorship from the Institute of Sport, which wasn't much, and then fundraising. Until FIFA decided to have a Women's World Cup, there was hardly any money in women's soccer before that '91 team was selected. We would have got a bigger grant and that type of stuff to go to the World Cup, you know, but we didn't go so, you know, it was always lamington drives, fundraising and all that.

> I played for Wenty Waratahs for a number of years and then we played state championships and I got in the NSW side. I think I was about 20 when I got selected in the Australian side, but we didn't tour, so I only played one season in the Australian-side women's soccer at that age. I was selected in the 1991 World Cup side.

The Australian coach at the time, Steve Darby, had only four days to prepare the team for the qualifying tournament. However, the ASF came on board with a late contribution of $5,000 to help the players cover costs, which improved the morale of the team leading into the first game.

Sharon was 26 when selected to play in the first of the qualifying games against New Zealand at Club Marconi in Sydney. Unfortunately, Australia lost the game one goal to nil. Australia then defeated New Zealand in the return match one goal to nil. Due to the results of the other games, Australia had to defeat PNG by 16 goals to progress through to the World Cup—they managed 12. And New Zealand won through as the Oceania Confederation's representative at the inaugural Women's World Cup in China in 1991.

> So we missed out, New Zealand went to the first Women's World Cup and we missed out and it was very disappointing. I just couldn't get over that, you know, we trained so hard to qualify. I was a little bit older than some of the younger ones, so they went on to the Olympics, but I retired. I just chose to retire because, I don't know, I couldn't get back into it.

The bitter disappointment of such a close call majorly impacted Sharon's future in the game.

> The disappointment of us not qualifying was heartbreaking. I continued to be selected in the team the following year and because the World Cup was another four years away, and I thought about the Olympics as well. We were going to be an invitation sport at the 1996 Olympics, but I couldn't get over the disappointment of missing out in the first Women's World Cup because we didn't qualify on goal average.

While Sharon decided to leave women's football, she continued representing Australia in the indoor game for some years.

> I mean I only retired from outdoor. I still continued to play indoor soccer and my last tour for indoor was to Canada, and we won. (Laughter.) So I retired on a winning note in the end. I was 32.

The disappointment of not qualifying was not the only reason Sharon retired. Like many women in football, she had to face the age-old question of focusing on a career and financial security or continuing with the game that she loved but that provided little financial support and no future outside of sport.

> Well, you couldn't really hold a full-time job because of the intense training and then going down to the Institute of Sport whenever they called you up to train before we went overseas. Basically, I didn't work a full-time job until later on in life, and that was part of my decision to retire as well. Will I go for the Olympics, or will I go and get a full-time job and get a mortgage? I chose the full-time job and the mortgage.

One of the few alternatives available to the women players was to chase the limited financial rewards being offered by the more professional football leagues internationally.

> In '91 I think the highest paid player was a girl called Hannah. She was an American player. I think she was getting maybe $80,000 from state sponsorships per year, but she was the highest. Basically, most of the girls had to go overseas, like Julie Murray, Julie Dolan, had to go overseas and play to get money from different overseas women's sides or even get selected in university sides in America.

Even if you were selected to represent your country, the financial support was limited, and most players struggled to meet the many requirements of training, working and playing. Many of the women had to compete with the need to earn a living or gain an education. The level of commitment required to play at a high level often at their own expense made it difficult for many to commit to the game full time.

Compounding the issue was the lack of recognition for the effort and dedication.

> I think it was only a government grant of about $100, $120 a week to a player for that '91 World Cup side. You can't live on that, you know. So it was a

struggle to go to work and then try and train full time as well and succeed in that and then get time off work, so you know, that was the struggle. Getting the name out there, and actually being recognised for representing your country because people didn't recognise it; they didn't understand women's soccer. What's that, you know?

After leaving the game, Sharon has had time to reflect on her time in the game and what her participation has meant to her.

I think, as I've got older, I've only realised how good you are, you know. I mean in the sense until you retire or you're out of the game for a while and older people come up to you and say, 'Jeez, you're a good player. I love watching you play,' and all this type of stuff. You don't realise that.

I did it because I loved my sport, plus I loved training and I wanted to make my mum and dad proud of me—that was my drive besides the love of the game. When we won against New Zealand and were back in the race to qualify for the World Cup, I'd never seen my dad cry, and he ran down to the fence, and he gave me the biggest hug he's ever given me and just handed me the Australian flag, and we ran across the field and it was just, yeah, I will never ever forget that.

Sharon is still occasionally invited to FFA functions and local international matches involving the Matildas. She is especially honoured to have received her commemorative cap as part of FFA's initiative to celebrate the history of the game by honouring individual players with a cap highlighting the player's debut game details and their Matildas number. However, she criticises how this recognition has not reached all of those who pioneered the game.

I got invited to the Hall of Fame presentation two years ago and, you know, there were a couple of the young Matildas there. But because I don't follow it so closely, I wouldn't know them if they walked past me in the street, and they probably wouldn't know us either. But it's good when you get invited to those things so you can mix and just talk about where we've come from to now. I'd love to take another 15 years off my life and do it all again and see what it's like now instead of the struggle that we had.

I think the biggest thing they brought in is the caps. You get a number for your cap for when you came into the league, but there's been controversy

> (over) that, where they're not recognising everyone. Like my caps began in the '91 World Cup side, not back when I was playing at 19. I played a few games against Sweden who came over, and they didn't recognise those.
>
> I mean, my number is 65, and so they say, okay, I was the 65th person to wear the green and gold jumper, where that's not right because I wore it back when I was 19. Some other players even missed out and didn't get a cap because they weren't recognised in that area. That's disappointing for the older people, back in the (day), probably my era was when it was all kind of turning around, developing and we were getting the World Cup. But a lot of people put a lot of sacrifices on the line back before that, just to represent and play against different countries and go over to different countries and play in these series. A lot of money was spent touring with that as well and that should have been, they should have been recognised, I thought.
>
> But there are women out there that did represent their country and weren't presented with a cap. I got mine, but a lot of people missed out and that's not fair. They all did the same training, same hard yards; they must have just drew a line in the sand and said anyone from this year on or anyone who toured in these teams—I don't know how they did it.

In 1997, Sharon was employed at the Sydney Harbour Casino as a security officer before being elevated to the positions of security supervisor, security duty manager and more recently security operations manager at the Star Casino. She attributes her leadership skills to her time spent playing football as a valued team member.

> My job at the moment is running a small team at the Star. I mean I'm an acting duty manager. If I didn't have the team environment or actually being—because I played defender—actually being able to organise people to get back on the ... you know, once they make a break and all that type of stuff ... that's helped me in my career. I'm the only female that's ever made it as far as an acting duty manager, and I just missed out on the manager's position there. That's because of my team involvement in soccer. I'm putting it down to that. To go to an incident like a fight or having to lock people down or remove people, to be able to look at the whole picture and instruct grown men to do this, do this, and they just take commands off me because I'm a leader. It's shown me how to lead in my life.

Looking back on her time in the game, Sharon is proud of her achievements and is thankful for the many friends she has made and still keeps in contact with. Just to be acknowledged by people who knew her as a footballer makes her day.

> I will always be proud that I've played for Australia, and whether it's soccer or ping pong. You get the sense that I think Packer quoted once—and that's not James, but his dad—quoted, 'I'd give away all my fortunes to wear a baggy green,' and that's true. Money can't buy you an Australian jersey, you have to earn it. It doesn't matter in what code you are, you still do the hard yards to get there, and you sacrifice things like work or friendships or relationships sometimes.
>
> I keep in contact with the friends I made and regularly just have drinks with them or whatever or catch up. With others just every now and then, you see them out, it's good to say hello and yeah, catch up. I developed a few friends in Queensland and catch up with them once a year or so. There are plenty of people out there, and I always know when I'm walking through the casino and someone yells out 'Youngy', because that was my nickname. Youngy was my soccer name so then I turn around, and I know it's someone from soccer because nobody at work calls me that. Yeah, so, it's interesting talking of that—apparently I haven't changed much. (Laughter.) So they still know me, yeah, it's good to see that as well.
>
> I'd never turn it back, mate. A great part of my life, and I tell you, if I could turn back time, I'd just do it all again. I would have no regrets of doing it all again.

12. Lisa Casagrande

I've had some fantastic, wonderful, irreplaceable and priceless experiences.

Lisa Casagrande is one of the most highly rated players to ever represent the far north coast of NSW. Lisa began her career playing for the Goonellabah Soccer Club (her only club team) with the boys' teams at the age of six and had a meteoric rise to the national team at 14.

On her way to national selection Lisa faced the hardships associated with women in football including lack of support and the failure of the game to recognise and acknowledge women in football. By the time she retired, Lisa had competed in two World Cups and had become the youngest player to reach 50 international caps while playing for Australia. She played 64 times for the Matildas, scoring 16 goals along the way (60 A internationals, 13 goals). In 2009, at the 125-year anniversary of Northern NSW Football she was named in the Northern NSW women's team of the era. In 2013, FFA named Lisa in the team of the decade for 1990–1999, and in 2015 Lisa was inducted into the FFA Hall of Fame.

Women's soccer launched on the far north coast of NSW in 1974 with foundation member Goonellabah Soccer Club joining Thistles, Richmond Rovers and Teachers College. By 1978, the competition had attracted teams from Ballina, Nimbin and another Lismore club, Italo Stars. After just two years, the women's team disbanded in 1977 after the tragic death of Callan McMillan (founding member of the club and of its women's football team), and it wasn't until 1990 that the club re-entered the women's competition with two teams, going on to win the grand final in 1991. Goonellabah has been part of the women's competition ever since, and central to its success and the development of the game in NSW in general was Lisa Casagrande.

Lisa was born in 1978 and began playing at six when her father signed her up with the Goonellabah Soccer Club.

> I became involved in women's football from a young age. I wanted to play competitive sports, from memory, netball, but I was too young. My father was a footballer, so I followed him around playing rugby league, and somehow because I couldn't get into netball he enrolled me into soccer, which was just up the road from where we used to live.
>
> My father was reasonably good at league. I think he tried out for Manly in Sydney and got accepted but missed home too much. He came from a big family of nine children and most of the boys did quite well. So you have that sporting background, and I guess that's probably what pushed me through the soccer periods.

Lisa started her playing career with the boys' teams and stayed with the Goonellabah club for most of her young career before getting selected in the state and then national representative teams. Although she enjoyed playing with the boys and credits her skill development to the higher level of competitiveness, the going got tough at times.

> I started off with the Goonellabah Soccer Club from under-six and played with the boys up until the under-16s. The boys were always fun because I started at a young age and most of them were always fine. It became difficult probably from the age of 13–14 onwards when the boys started to shoot up and become more like men—that was always difficult with my small stature.
>
> When I was about 14, I played both the women's and the boys' game. I played Division 1 on the Sunday and played with boys on the Saturday. I was only playing the women's game maybe one or two years, and I got selected in the state under-16s team. I then went to the national state under-19s titles, hoping to get into the under-19s team, and I got into the national team. Two weeks later I was off to Japan, my first game for Australia.
>
> So it was an escalated sort of introduction to the national team.

That was 1994, and Lisa was just 14. In the same year, she won a scholarship to the Australian Institute of Sport (AIS), where she trained with the men's team in preparation for the upcoming FIFA Women's World Cup in 1995.

> I went to the Australian Institute of Sport where I was the only female with the Australian Institute men's team in preparation for the World Cup in 1995. So I pretty well got into the national team, went to Japan, had a short period

at home, and then they took me to Canberra to train with the AIS boys in preparation for the World Cup in 1995.

During 1998–1999, Lisa played for Canberra Eclipse in the National Women's Soccer League where she was the top scorer.

Australia qualified for the second FIFA Women's World Cup, held in Sweden in 1995. The national team represented the Oceania Football Confederation (OFC), with Lisa scoring Australia's only goal against the USA. Unfortunately, Australia lost that game four goals to one, and all other pool games, to finish last of the 12 competing nations.

Not letting the experience dissuade her, Lisa continued in the national team and was again selected as part of the squad for the 1999 FIFA Women's World Cup in the USA. She was 21 and played every game of the tournament. The Matildas represented the OFC after defeating New Zealand in the qualifying games; however, after drawing the first game against Ghana lost the remaining pool games to finish in 11th position. The team was still to record a World Cup victory, but notching up their first tournament point was considered an improvement on 1995.

Australia was now in its final preparations for the Sydney 2000 Olympic Games. But the team were suffering from a lack of media attention on top of the general lack of financial support for women. That and the fact they were often left to train in second-hand gear led them to the infamous nude calendar.

> Yes, many participated (I was not involved) in the naked calendar back in 2000. The calendar certainly gained national publicity. In doing so, this increased the awareness of the national women's team to the broader society.

Lisa was selected as an alternate player in the Olympic Games squad but didn't play because of injury.

> I had my sesamoid bone removed out of my foot and it was never the same after that. I was unable to sprint at the same speed as prior to the injury.

The Matildas failed to progress beyond the pool games after losing to Germany, the eventual silver medallists, and Brazil. But they eked out a draw against Sweden. During this period, Lisa was offered a scholarship in the USA. Men's USA Olympic Coach Clive Charles invited her to join the University of Portland team. She competed in the National College Athletic Association (NCAA) competition, which comprised 274 teams.

> The University of Portland coaches saw me at the 1995 World Cup in Sweden, and offered me a scholarship. Initially I didn't accept the scholarship due to the fear of leaving and living in another country. After a game at the USA 1999 World Cup, the Portland coaches took me to the college and showed me around. I loved the college, coaches and players and the decision became extremely easy to return there and live.

Lisa moved to Portland Oregon in 1999–2001 to complete a master's degree and play in the college system with the University of Portland Pilots. Lisa spent three and a half years in the USA where she made many friends and has fond memories of her time spent there before returning to Australia in 2002.

Lisa didn't have time to start a career as her football career took off from a very young age.

> I amazingly completed an undergrad degree while I was training at the AIS in Canberra, while working casually to support myself and being involved as full-time player at the AIS.

After returning to Australia Lisa decided to quit; the foot injury had stolen her speed, and her experiences in the USA led her to question her place in the Matildas. Lisa retired from the international game at 22 but returning to club football was not an option.

By the time she retired, Lisa had competed in two World Cups and had become the youngest player to reach 50 international caps while playing for Australia in the Algarve Cup in Portugal in 1999. She played 64 times for the Matildas in sum, scoring 13 goals along the way. In 2009, Lisa received her Matildas commemorative cap at the 125-year anniversary of Northern NSW Football where she was also named in the Northern NSW women's team of the era. In 2013, FFA named Lisa in the team of the decade for 1990–1999, and in 2015 Lisa was inducted into the FFA Hall of Fame.

> I am grateful for the opportunity to have had the experiences, to travel and play in front of large crowds in big stadiums, and meet and play with some wonderful people. I was able to visit many countries around the world and have a taste of many cultures during my career.

Lisa also expresses her frustration at how many in the wider game fail to understand or acknowledge the history of women in football, seeming oblivious to the differences between the men's and women's game.

> During my playing career there was a significant difference between male and female national teams regarding program funding and support. As time has progressed it is delightful to see less of a disparity.

On the far north coast of NSW, the Lisa Casagrande Medal is now awarded to the best female player of each year's grand final.

> It is an honour to have the far north coast medal awarded in my name. My sincere wishes for the future of all female soccer players and programs on the far north coast.

13. Belinda Wilson

We all want to be a part of the Olympics when we're kids, and I still remember as a five-year-old watching the Olympics for the very first time and turning around to Mum and (saying), 'I want to be there one day.'

Belinda Wilson is Byron Bay's favourite daughter—arguably the highest profile and successful female sportsperson ever to come from the famous town.

Belinda started playing football at the age of 11 with the Byron Bay Soccer Club; however, she soon found that coaching was where she belonged. Belinda has made a career in coaching both women and men, but her successes clearly relate to her role as a coach and mentor in women's football. Coaching has taken Belinda all over the world, including Norway, Sweden, Denmark, Guam and Australia, with a stint in the W-League with Brisbane Roar. Belinda has held a number of highly ranked administrative roles with FFA, AFC and FIFA. In December 2020, Belinda assumed the role of Senior Technical Development Manager with FIFA and is working with the Women's Football Division in Zurich.

Belinda has achieved in an area where females historically have suffered at the hands of the male-dominated hierarchies, facing discrimination, which often led to women disengaging with this area of football.

Byron Bay was involved in the development of football on the far north coast region of New South Wales from the beginning. The beachside town competed in informal games against neighbouring teams from Nashua, Federal, Bangalow and Mullumbimby throughout the deep rural depression of the 1930s. Yet a formal team was long coming—it was 1963 when the Byron Bay Soccer Club first entered junior teams in the Brunswick Byron competition, and the club joined the larger Lismore District only in 1982.

Women's football was reportedly played informally in Byron Bay during the 1960s and 1970s, yet no team was affiliated with the club. It wasn't until 1997 that the first women's team emerged there when they competed in third division that year. Since then, Byron Bay FC have created a proud history in women's football, with the women's program being the first team in the club to win a major Football Far North Coast title. And in 1998, the senior women's and first grade under-16s teams both won the Pointscore Championship and were unbeaten throughout the season. The team, known as the Zebras, went on to win the region's pre-season cup competition, the Callan McMillan Shield, three times in the 2000s.

Belinda Wilson was born in 1975 in Sydney; however, the family moved to Byron Bay in 1977. In July of that same year, the Far North Coast Women's Amateur Soccer Association (FNCWSA) was formed to manage the growth of the women's game. Previous to that, the first recognised competition for women had begun in 1974 with teams from Thistles, Rovers, Teachers College and Goonellabah competing. The teams were made up of mostly high school girls, college students or women who were involved with their brothers, sons, husbands or partners—all had to be at least 12 years of age.

Belinda began her playing career with the Byron Bay Soccer Club when she was only 11, and she was to go on to become one of Australia's most respected coaches and one of Byron Bay's most successful football exports.

> I first started playing when I was about eight or nine. I wanted to play football. My best friend was playing football, and I would go and watch him play. I wanted to be involved, and his mum and dad were involved in the Melbourne Football Club. But back in those days girls couldn't play with boys. I still wanted to play at the age of nine, 10 and 11, and through the same family their eldest daughter was playing football with a local club, Byron Bay Women's Football Club. It was a senior team, playing in the Premier Division, the top division in Lismore, and they allowed me to play for them, and I think I was 11.

After just one year in a player's strip, Belinda decided that the game wasn't for her. However, discussions between her mum, brother and the Byron Bay Soccer Club would ensure that Belinda was not lost to the game and her destiny to one day represent her country was set in motion.

> So I played a season, a season and a half, and then I went, 'I don't want to play.' It was no more fun, none of my friends were playing. So I went to high school and then it was my younger brother, he wanted to play football. He was five or six, and he went down to the local club and signed up. I came home from school, and he turned around and said, 'You're my coach,' and I

said, 'No, I'm not.' I think I was 15, and he goes, 'Yes you are, I signed you up.' Vlad Knaus, the president of the Byron Bay Soccer Club, had spoken to my mum saying that they needed a coach for the team and between my brother and my mum they kind of signed me up as well.

I turned around and said, 'Well, I've got better things to do on a Saturday morning,' but then I went down and saw the kids and played a little bit of football. I had no idea of how to coach the game but just played some fun games and enjoyed it, and it kind of went from there.

The opportunities for women in coaching football in Australia were limited at the time. Those interested in coaching roles often faced institutional barriers and obstacles from the male-dominated clubs and associations. Belinda was fortunate to have the support of her family, friends and the local club.

> My mum and family were always supportive in terms of what I wanted to do. It didn't matter what. Mum saw that my brother and I were hanging out and I was looking after him, so Mum had no issues. My sisters had no issues. When I was 16, 17, some of my friends at school would take the mickey out of me. They were always like, 'What are you doing Saturday morning, why are you never able to come out with us and hang out with us and stuff? Why are you always going to football?' It's because I enjoyed it, I loved it.
>
> When I was 18 and going out to the pub and obviously in the early hours of the morning if football was on television, and I'm watching the football instead of discussing whatever's going on at that point of time in terms of conversation, they'd go, 'What are you doing?'—'I'm watching the football. Why? Because I like it, and it's that hour of the morning when I can watch it.'
>
> While I was studying at university and it became a little more serious and I was giving up a lot of my time in terms of travelling and coaching, other people started questioning, 'Why are you doing that, you're never going to earn a living from it, you should just focus on this, you should focus on that.' So yeah, some questioned why I did it, and they are probably the only ones out of my friends who were a little bit negative in terms of my involvement.
>
> But everyone else supported me—said it was a great thing: 'You're really good around kids, you should become a teacher.' It's really easy when kids are motivated, that's why it's good. I don't do well with unmotivated kids— back then. Now to do what I've done and to travel and kind of make a career out of it, now it's those same people who were quite negative who have kind

of flipped and went, 'Oh, oh, okay.' But I think they were trying to just look out for me because they saw no real future in it.

After learning her trade with the boys' teams, Belinda moved to coaching the women at the Byron Bay club and then had an opportunity to develop her coaching skills as an elite coach of women's representative teams.

> I coached the boys for about seven years, until I was 21, 22. It was a mixed team. There were some girls involved, and then my brother and I had more arguments on the field regarding stuff that was going on at home. He didn't brush his teeth or whatever, so it started to affect his game and obviously the team. And in fact, it affected me so I kind of went, 'We're parting ways. I need to find you guys a new coach,' and from there I went into the women's comp for Byron and also at that same time I was introduced to representative football for the girls. Peter Ware (head coach of the Premier Division men's team) asked me to go and interview in Lismore at far north coast for the under-14s Far North Coast women's representative team.

In 1998, at 23, Belinda took control of the Far North Coast women's representative team. Two years later, she was integral in developing the Byron Bay Soccer Club women's team and from there coached state teams. Her coaching eventually led to a stint with the NSW Institute of Sport under Alan Stajcic's squad. Yet Belinda's destiny was again tested when she found herself unemployed in Newcastle.

> I was still coaching the women's team back in Byron, but then I was also coaching not only representatives from Far North Coast but then also asked to coach state teams. Originally, I was asked to start as an assistant, but the head coach at the time, Renee Iserief, had to pull out, and then they asked me to step in as the head coach, so it's kind of a flow-on effect from there.
> I did my various badges up until then with the support of the club and the support of Northern NSW. I then moved to Newcastle in 2001 or 2002. My brother got asked to play for the Newcastle United youth team, so it was easier for me to transfer to Newcastle University than it was for Mum and everyone to live down there, so me and my brother moved down. Then from there, I was asked to do the Prime team, which was a State League team. It was Newcastle-based, so we played in Sydney every week in the Super League. I also moved up from the under 14s to be the head coach of the 17s/18s team.

In 2003, I had to make a decision. I had to finish my degree. I started it in 1997 so it was late, and I had two subjects to go. My brother had moved back to Byron due a good mate of his pass(ing) away tragically and (him having) pretty much a career-ending injury, so he went back to Byron, and I was kind of in Newcastle going, 'Well, there is no real reason for me to stay here.'

I had to get my degree finished back in Lismore and then from there decide what I wanted to do. It was like, 'I'm not going to get a job in football.' I was working with Northern NSW, I was doing an internship, and I thought that would lead into an administrative role. It didn't, so I was stuck.

I decided to join the Ambulance to finish my degree—did my training for seven weeks down in Sydney, and then, while I was down there, the Ambulance kept on delaying when the classes started, so I was not working so I was on unemployment and had to go and look for jobs each week. And then there was an advertisement. I think it was on sportspeople.com—Soccer NSW looking for a Female Participation Officer. So anyway, I didn't hear anything from Soccer NSW for a few weeks and about the third or fourth week in the training, I get a phone call wanting an interview, and I was like, 'I can't. I'm not free between here and here because I'm in class, I'm in with the Ambulance at the moment. If you want to interview me, it would have to be after hours.' So, I had the interview and about three or four days later they rang me up and offered me the job.

Then I was like, 'What do I do?' So then I phoned Ken Kaiser (Director of Coaching at Northern NSW Soccer Federation) because at that time I considered him a mentor. But he said I'd already decided because he goes, 'What have you been doing, where have you been working yourself up to, and where are you now?' So I took the opportunity, and I was involved with females as an administrator, but obviously I love my coaching so within that role I decided, okay, from nine to five I was an administrator, and from five to nine in the evening I was a coach. So I got involved with Alen Stajcic's NSWIS squad. I was his assistant for two years, and then I got involved with the Super League with Marconi and I started coaching the under-12s team.

Belinda's role as a Football Female Participation Officer with Soccer NSW became untenable after the organisation let the second officer go and did not replace them. The workload became unbearable, with Belinda working 60-hour weeks and coaching after hours. So Belinda took a punt and asked a question, one that would change the direction of her coaching life.

> I walked over to Alistair Edwards—he was the head coach of the national under-19s at the time—and just asked, 'Are you looking for a full-time assistant?' Knowing that his role was only part time, but (it was) just one of those smart-arse, get-me-out-of-here kind of things, and he said, 'Funnily enough, there is a position over in Kuala Lumpur (KL) in Malaysia.' I've gone, 'Where's that?' I don't know, I'm from Byron; I have my own little world. And then he goes, 'If you're interested, it's for women's football,' and I said something like, 'Anything to get me out of this situation.'
>
> And then within that week I had two other people also quiz me about that. I'd thought they'd all spoken to each other because they were in the same circles, but apparently, they didn't. I applied (and), surprisingly, considering I knew who was also going for the role, I got the job and pretty much within that month I was in KL.

Belinda started in KL as the coach education manager for women's football in 2006. She was later appointed Acting Director of Women's Football for the Asian Football Confederation (AFC) in the same year, staying until January 2009.

> I came in fairly naïve, but I learned a lot in those two and a half years in terms of how it worked at the very top, from an administrator's point of view, and then got jack of that after so many, many issues.
>
> I hadn't been exposed to some of the politics or the workings of the upper echelon of power in football or any sport. So, to walk in with this very passionate, want-to-do-the-right-thing-for-the-lowest-level, then come to realise they don't care about all that was very confronting. I started to learn that, through my time there and towards the end, I kind of worked it out and I kind of went, ouch! The fact also that the women's game in particular wasn't very well supported, although they'd turn around and say, 'Yes we have this,' and, 'Yes we have that,' but really there was no support.
>
> There was never a time we as a department would go forward with an idea to help the development or to help to better the competitions. We were always knocked back, and the biggest reason was always the budget. And then you hear they're spending millions and millions of dollars on the men's Asian cup and then we have a budget of $750,000, and that lack of respect. Same level of competition, but you know what, we really don't care, there's some money to help you get along, do what you can with it, but all the focus is on the men's game. The attitude was cultural as well because at the time, a Qatari representative was involved in running the game.

Mohammed bin Hammam was a Qatari and president of the AFC from 2002 until 2011 and a member of FIFA's executive committee from 1996 until 2011. In 2012, the FIFA Ethics Committee banned him for life from all FIFA-related football activities. The Court of Arbitration for Sport overturned this decision later that year due to a lack of evidence. However, only five months later, bin Hammam was again in the news when FIFA handed out its second life ban for 'repeated violations of the ethics code on conflicts of interest'. Bin Hamman resigned from all football-related duties prior to the announcement of the second FIFA life ban.

> Mohammed bin Hammam, or el presidente. He came across as very supportive of women's football by creating a women's department, by creating competitions, by creating some pathways, but it was very superficial. There were no layers underneath that, and then everything was steered towards what can we do for the men's and how can we do it better.
>
> But every time we had an issue there was no support. And then as I took control of the department, the support got less and less because obviously I moved up the rank but then no one was filling in my spot. He specifically wanted a female-only department, so even if I had, and I did, any male colleagues who were in the women's game (and) were very passionate about (the) women's game and could do a good job, a lot better than I could because of their experience, I wasn't allowed to employ them. So then you had a gender bias.
>
> They don't care, it doesn't register because they don't have those rules in their country. So the fact (was) that for 12 months I was the Director of Women's Football and I had no one for women's football development. I had no one for coach education. I had one person for competitions, and I had a secretary and that was it because we'd also lost during that year the person who was involved with referees. So as director, I had to cover three positions plus the director role and also monitor and make sure the competition was running.

The AFC consists of 47 member nations, but not all have women's teams. Since its inception in 1975, the AFC Asian Women's Cup has grown to include 21 competing nations at the qualifying games for the 2018 tournament, which was held in Jordan for the first time.

> So when it came down to the crunch, that's what killed it for me. And the other stuff that was happening in and around just added more fuel in terms of

why I shouldn't be doing the role. To this day, I still get asked to go back, and I was told yesterday that you should never, ever close the door, and I said to AFC, 'The door will always be closed, and that's because of the experience that I had there.'

Belinda realised that she needed a break: 'I started to change as a person.'

Then a mutual friend introduced me to a mate living in Norway, Scandinavia. It was at a grassroots conference, and then he said, 'Make sure you catch up with my mate in Prague,' and then I caught up with him, and we got along. I said, 'I can't believe you're from Australia living in Sweden for x amount of years and you've never come to Byron.' Because every Swedish person has come to Byron, so with that, he came to Byron for New Year's and then that week he offered me a job—coaching role. I had said no at that point due to the fact that I had just got the role as the Director of Women's Football, so I was like, 'No, no, I'm now Director of Women's Football.'

That was in January, and I was given the role in November. About February I'd emailed him back and said, 'Is that offer still there because I'm interested—it's not working out for me.'

I didn't hear from him for months and then when I was at the 2008 Asian Cup in Vietnam, I got an email from him saying, 'If you want it, it's yours.' So with that I replied, 'Yep, definitely, and I'm heading over to Spain in September on my way back to KL. I could stop and catch up with you in Sweden and we can work out the bits and pieces.' And then I went there in September, and he told me about the scope of the job. At that point, I wasn't sure where I was going to be living, whether it was going to be Denmark, Sweden or Norway, but I was at a point where I didn't really care, and it was an opportunity to coach full time. That happened in September 2008. I resigned from the AFC when I came back from Spain (January 2009).

Everyone was saying, 'It's career suicide,' and I said, 'I don't care. You don't understand my lifestyle, you don't understand where I've grown up, I don't care. It's not about the money or the power or the prestige, it's about the lifestyle.'

And so, with them asking me to change my mind and stuff like that, I was fairly adamant: 'No, thank you very much.' I knew I'd made the right decision when they almost refused me to go back for a dear friend's funeral, and in fact I missed his funeral because of that. They thought that football was more important than what was going on in my life, so it was very upsetting at the time, so I went back to do the right thing by them as an employee. I wasn't happy in the last six weeks I had there. I left with a rather stale taste in my mouth.

I was supposed to start in Norway in January 2009, but thankfully my boss was a little bit smart and said, 'Don't come yet, it's too cold.' So we started in April 2009, and I just pretty much hung out in Byron for four months.

I was the head coach for a company called Coerver in Oslo, where we would go from club to club and we would do academy-style coaching focusing on individual technique, and we did camp scenarios as well: weekend camps, summer camps, winter camps. So I did that for three years and just fell in love with coaching again—fell in love with football again and found myself again in terms of who I was and why I was doing it and, yeah, just got that passion back.

From a footballing sense it was fantastic to live, breathe and just to see it every day. People in the street (were) talking about football, it's in the paper, it's on the television, it's all around you so you're just in depth with it. You know what's going on in the world of football, in the different leagues that are shown. So from a learning point of view, to learn the culture of Europe, to learn different styles of football because you can see it was an amazing experience for me. And then to coach—and this is the first time I'd become a technical coach—and then to coach specifically technique and not the game was interesting as well because it was one area of my own education that I wasn't focused on. It made me rethink how I approach my coaching and how I approach things in general.

And then to teach young kids who struggle with the language, the English language was an experience in itself. Even though they're taught English from the first day in school, it was the accent they they've had major problems with. I don't know why, but within a year I kind of noticed a bit of a pattern with the younger kids, and parents would come up and say, 'Oh my child keeps crying, he doesn't understand, he seems to be struggling.' I would say, 'If you give your child three weeks and if he's still struggling, then it's not the sport for him, but after three weeks you see them settling down.' I said, 'Just let him stay or her stay and she'll be fine.' It was like a three-week teething course: (a) they're getting used to me. (b) they're getting used to the discipline because Norwegians don't have discipline. Scandinavians don't have discipline. They're allowed to do whatever they want. There's no set boundaries. And (c) it's language. By a year or so, I had some of the language, especially from the coaching point of view, pretty much worked out, but still with the accent and the pronunciation, it wasn't quite right, so the kids didn't quite understand. Most parents were good, but some took their children away.

Then I got sick of the winters, the minus 25s, the 20-hour darkness. So I was like, 'So I love the job, love everything we do but I just want to go home. It's been seven years since I've been in Australia.' So in April 2012, I came home and didn't do anything.

During my time with AFC and while I was in Norway, I started to work with FIFA for the women's game as an instructor. I would go to various countries and do basic level, intermediate level or advanced level coaching courses for a lot of the countries. It was all about development, so it wasn't all about teaching the national teams, it was basically starting at the grassroots level.

Belinda signed on with FIFA back in 2007 as a coach instructor conducting women's coaching courses throughout the member associations and then in 2019 as a technical consultant in women's football. She also did technical reports for FIFA at the 2007 and 2011 FIFA Women's World Cups and the 2008 Olympic Games in Beijing.

For both the World Cup and the Olympics, I was there as a technical study member and that was through my involvement with the AFC. Originally, I was supposed to go as an observer because I wanted to see how the technical study worked so that we could bring that back into AFC competitions, but then that turned into an actual place within the technical study group.

I still remember sitting around the roundtable and everyone introducing themselves. It was pretty intimidating; by the time they got to me, I hadn't played for Australia, and I'd been involved in the women's game for a while but at a very, very grassroots level compared to these girls. So in that environment it was—the only reason I'm here is because of a political reason. AFC wanted someone to represent them, but if it had been the men's game it would have been total shutdown. But in the women's game, especially at the moment they saw that, they identified with it, and they took me under their wing, and until this day those relationships are still there, and I chat to them every other week regarding different football scenarios.

They're the ones who told me I should go home and start coaching a team and push myself. So yeah a lot of support from that and then the Olympic

Games. I mean, we all want to be a part of the Olympics when we're kids, and I still remember as a five-year-old watching the Olympics for the very first time and turning around to Mum and (saying), 'I want to be there one day.' It was as an athlete, but that didn't work out so to be there, to be a part of it, to be involved with it and to see it, it's an amazing experience. That's how all the BS that I went through in terms of in the administration and whatever hardships I've had, it didn't matter at that point in time because of that experience, to be there. I still remember walking down the Great Wall of China and running into the Australian diving team and just seeing Australia written on the back of the shirts, knowing that I was at the Olympics, it was just fantastic.

Just a young girl coming from Byron Bay who had an interest in football being in that environment was mind-blowing. I was amongst some of the best female and male coaches within the game, and to be sitting in a room full of female coaches at that time who had not only represented their country as players but also as coaches and won major tournaments was unbelievable.

So when I came back to Australia in 2012, I said to FIFA that I had nothing on over the next x amount of months, 12 months, depending on when I get a job, so if you need anyone I'm available. Previous to that, I'd only done one or two a year for FIFA, whether that was a technical study or a coach instruction, and then last year I did seven trips. I was employed earning some money, so I didn't really need to go out and look for a job, so it kind of worked out.

When I was in Japan for the under-20s as a coach/instructor for an advanced level, I got an email from FFA. It was sent out to a few people regarding the job in Brisbane with Football Queensland for the high-performance coach of the women's program with the W-League team, so it was a dual role in that respect. Prior to that, I'd also applied for the Sydney job, the Wanderers position, but I never got the job. I didn't really want it because I really didn't want to relocate to Sydney. I'd expressed that to a few people at FFA. They'd offered me the assistant role and I said, 'Look, to relocate to Sydney, find somewhere to live, to find a job that's flexible enough for me to do the assistant role, it's too hard, thank you but no thank you.'

So when this job came out, it was a no-brainer really. Being in Brisbane it was only a few hours from home, and it's in the area that pretty much I'd want to stay in. But to come in as a first-time coach in the W-League to coach a team that's been in four finals, and they've won two major premierships, there was a lot of pressure. And I really didn't think that I would get it because of the lack of my qualifications in Australia and the lack of my experience coaching teams at that level.

I got back from Japan on the Wednesday, and the following day is when I had the interview and then on the Saturday I got a phone call from the CEO at Football Queensland saying I had the position. I hadn't really stopped since then, so that was the beginning of September.

Then I met the team, and then I had to go to Pakistan for ten days. So I got the job, came in on the Wednesday to speak to FFA, sorry to Football Queensland, signed the paperwork, then the girls were at training on Thursday, so then I came back Thursday night, met the girls for the very first time and said, 'Hi, I'm Belinda Wilson, I'm now the coach of the Football Queensland and the W-League team. Unfortunately, on Saturday I'm leaving to go to Pakistan for 10 days so I'll catch up with you when I get back.'

So I observed the training session, observed the two assistant coaches who I now have, kind of went, okay, and then disappeared to Pakistan to do a course I couldn't get out of. And then I came back and kind of went, I've got two or three weeks to go till we start the W-League, and we had some major issues with the squad numbers. A lot of the players had left because Football Queensland had left the announcement of the coach too late so players were being scouted and poached. So yeah, it was an interesting start—a lot of pressure at the beginning.

Belinda began as the Women's Football High Performance Manager at the Queensland Academy of Sport (QAS) and head coach of the Brisbane Roar women's W-League team in September 2012 through to September 2016. In her first season as coach, the team won the premier's plate and were runners-up to Sydney FC in the grand final. The team followed that up with semi-final appearances in seasons 2013–14 and 2015–16.

During her stay in Brisbane, Belinda served as the U/17 women's national team head coach during 2012–13 and coached the team at the U/17 World Cup qualifying games in China.

During her time at the Australian Institute of Sport, Belinda noticed that although women's football was developing and being recognised, there still remained pockets of resistance to change. Being relegated to the backfield was a common occurrence for many women's teams, but at a national level?

And an example of that was at the AIS with one field in particular. We couldn't use that field, that was for the AIS boys and the AIS boys only. And I was like, hang on a minute, we're a national team. We're under-17s, but we're still a national team so we should be above the AIS boys. So why can't we use that field, especially when it's not being used? Why do we have to go out in the crap field? So the standards, although they're getting better, they're still sometimes not.

Belinda spent a total of years coaching in the W-League and is a great supporter of the competition. However, she believes that it hasn't been given the respect that it deserves. The structure of the W-League is an ongoing issue within women's football to this day. The new professional leagues organisation, which was formed towards the end of 2020, has apparently agreed that changes do need to be made to the structure of the league to enable the competition to remain effective and compete internationally with other professional leagues worldwide.

It's not a true league, eight teams 12 games, there is nowhere in the world and there is nowhere else in Australia where that happens in a league structure. You're playing two rounds, you play everyone twice, and I think that's the biggest challenge in terms of what Australian women's football has. If you're going to do something for the women, have a bit of respect for it and treat it as you would any other competition. So just with that, I think that's the biggest challenge, just having equal respect, especially when it comes to the national competition. Because you don't have it at grassroots and you don't have it at state level, but at the national level where the standards are supposed to be set, we've said it's okay for women's football not to have a true league and that says a lot for everyone else who's trying to their best to promote women's football.

After leaving Brisbane Roar in 2016, Belinda took on a new coaching challenge when she again left Australia and travelled to Guam to be the technical director and women's national head coach for the Guam Football Association. She spent two years in Guam before returning to Australia in 2019 where she has become a member of the executive committee of Football Coaches Australia (FCA). This committee represents the many people involved in coaching in Australian football, including the W-League.

Belinda has now come full circle after recently being appointed head coach of Byron Bay Football Club from 2020, becoming the first woman coach of a Football Far North Coast (FFNC) Premier League club. It seems fitting she has now returned to the club that supported her when she first began her journey in coaching women's football. She balances her duties there with her role as a women's football consultant with FIFA. Reflecting on her lifelong passion, she said:

> It's the game, it challenges me in so many different ways now that without it my life would be rather boring. Although I'd probably open myself up to other areas and be challenged in that, at the moment I get so much out of a problem and solving that problem. But then I can also relate it back to life in itself, and that's where I think it's why I have so much passion about it because I can see the relationship. If I can't do it through one door then I can try and open another door and that's kind of how it is in terms of life, so I can relate the two together. I think that's where I enjoy it.

She also spoke of how her experiences abroad enabled her to reflect on the home game.

> Looking at Australia from afar, it was very interesting because we're very narrow-minded, not all of us, but a lot of us, and we're very egotistical. So to see that and then go, 'Wow, am I like that?' I hope I'm not, and then kind of change the way I see things and perceive things and conversations that you have and just remember to be a little bit more open-minded. I think the two kind of work together at the moment for me.
>
> But just that life experience that I've got from the game, it's been amazing, and I could never replace that, and football has given me that opportunity. I don't think if I had have stayed as an ambulance officer I would have had that same perception, or I wouldn't be sitting here today saying I've done that, or I've done this, or I've learnt this. It's been awesome.

14. Nicky Leitch

I did my qualification with Ange Postecoglou. So you look at the level that Ange is coaching now and I go, you know what, I can coach like he can, and I could still coach like he can except he's a man and he's got a pathway and a job opportunity, and I'm a woman and I don't.

Nicky Leitch (formerly Azzato) enjoyed a long and successful career in women's football as both a player and coach during the 1990s and 2000s. Nicky pioneered the role of women in coaching roles having to fight hard to be recognised and acknowledged in the historically male-dominated area of coaching during a time when women rarely attempted to enter the space.

Nicky is still involved today with her husband's goalkeeping academy.

Nicky Leitch was a late starter to the game. Born in 1967 and living in Reservoir in suburban Melbourne when I interviewed her, she says she didn't begin playing until her mid-20s. But in just four years she had progressed from club to national level, and she would go on to pioneer women's coaching in Victoria. It was thanks to her husband and family that Nicky took up the indoor version of the game. The added support and security migrant communities provided through their love of the game may have helped Nicky feel comfortable and accepted as a woman playing a male-dominated sport.

> I was married to an Italian, and I had six brothers-in-law and we used to play indoor soccer together. I was a late bloomer, and I didn't play junior football at all and so I was in my mid-20s. I was playing indoor soccer with my in-laws because I could play a bit, and the guy referring the indoor game said to me, 'You should play women's football', and I laughed. I went, 'Girls don't play football, what are you talking about?' And he said, 'No, no, they do.' So he connected me with a club, and I think I was about 25 when I started playing.

That's where I met Jason and then Betty and Mick Hoar (in 1992), and that's where I cut my teeth in outdoor women's football. Doxa (Glenroy Dockside) United—Betty played there occasionally and Mick was the coach. I played there for two years, winning the Best and Fairest—it was in Division 2, so if I was going to progress my soccer, I had to move up to a Division 1 team.

Over the years, Betty and Mick remained friends and I ended up working on the Victoria Women's Soccer Association (VWSA) with both of them. Mick also coached me in the state team a couple of times. Mick was the assistant coach the year Victoria beat Queensland for the national title, and I scored the winning goal in the final.

It wasn't uncommon for young girls to disguise themselves as boys during the 1970s to play sports that were historically men only. The Victorian Amateur Soccer Football Association (VASFA) forbade girls from boys' teams in 1960, only allowing them to play up until the U/11s in Victoria in 1980.

I lived in a street full of boys, so I grew up having a kick with them. When I was about 10 or 11, a group of us were having a kick at the local park (footy club) and the footy coach wanted to recruit me. He got our address, and when he came around to recruit me, he didn't realise I was a girl. He was shocked. What we did was a little bit shifty in that he recruited me as a boy and I played in the U/11 team for almost an entire season, until we played against a number of my school friends, who of course knew I was a girl. They dobbed me in, and before I knew it I wasn't allowed to play anymore. All I was allowed to do was run the boundary and train with my teammates. The footy club did offer to challenge me not being able to play, but the league wouldn't budge on the matter. A couple of years later, when I had turned 13, the league made a ruling that girls could play up to U/11s. It was too late for me.

I came from an AFL background as well, and I was very lucky I had a sporting background and a granddad who took me to all the sports I wanted to play. I desperately wanted to be a boy and play football. I played football in an under-11s team and very successfully won the Best and Fairest, and it was a church team and when they found out I was a girl I had to give the award back and I wasn't allowed to play anymore. So try and explain that to a 10-year-old.

I then ran the boundary line for AFL, so I was very sporty, and I was really good with coordination and ball skills, you know. I just kicked the ball with my mates and stuff. And as I said, I was in my early 20s really when my brothers-in-law conned me into playing soccer and because I was the best player in their team, even though I was a girl, they were like, 'You're playing with us.' I played tennis, and I played cricket and I did all of those things at a reasonably good level and it was only the referee of that indoor game who got me connected. So I should really thank him. (Laughter.)

Nicky found her family's support paramount in providing the necessary strength and resources to play, as was the case for so many women. But the high-level game took its toll on her relationships.

I'm really lucky my family were always really supportive. As I said, my granddad when he was alive would cart me around everywhere. I think Mum and Dad (too), and when I was older, I was driving so I could get myself to and from, and then I was married so my poor husband was very supportive because he had to (be) if he wanted to spend time with me. He was sporty as well, and we played indoor in some mixed teams and things like that, but ironically the football is probably what drove us apart in the end. I mean I was travelling a lot. When you get picked in the state teams and then in the Australian team, there are camps and different things. In the indoor team, I used to actually get on a bus Friday night, travel up to Sydney, train and stay with my teammates in Sydney on the weekend, come home on the bus Sunday night and then go to work. I did that fairly consistently for a while, so I think you know my marriage kind of got to a point where the football won ahead of the marriage, and we went our separate ways.

Nicky had always assumed that if you were good enough, the state selectors would come looking for you. But she had only been playing at Doxa for a year when she was encouraged to try out for state selection—she was picked for Victoria.

I spent two years at the lower division club, and then when I got involved with the state team I needed to be playing in the highest division, so I moved to what was called the Nunawading Club in 1990–1992. I was playing with better players, stronger players. That helped me. I was also playing indoor soccer at the same time I was playing outdoor soccer.

I first got picked for the team after my performance in Queensland at the Open National Championships in 1992. This is where Victoria beat Queensland,

and I scored the winning goal in the final. I was also the leading goal scorer in that tournament. So I went from being a bench player, to being in the first 11, to scoring the winning goal in the final and being awarded the leading goal scorer, to then being picked in the national team. It was an amazing week for me ... I just had a tournament where it all went right for me. So for me, the year that happened was incredibly significant and memorable, and I also got a tour with the Australian Indoor Team so it just all happened all at once, which is great.

After leaving Nunawading, Nicky went to South Melbourne to join the club's first women's team in 1992. She left two years later in 1994.

The disappointing thing for me with South Melbourne was we were sort of, we're the pioneers of South Melbourne but there's no recognition of (that), or history or anything.

Nicky played for Australia during the 1990s, a time in which the game was rapidly changing. On the international front the women's game had successfully held its inaugural Women's World Cup in 1991, followed by the Atlanta Olympic Games in 1996 and was looking forward to the upcoming Sydney-based Olympic Games in 2000. By the end of the decade, Nicky was moving into coaching.

There was a funding injection leading up to the 2000 Olympics, and really I was probably getting to the point where I was in my 30s and I was really too old to be in the Australian team then. From the age of 26 to about 30, I was involved with the national team, and when they got their funding for the Sydney Olympics, I then went more into coaching. I was involved with both the Victorian state teams and the Australian Outdoor Team in a coaching perspective rather than as a player.

At the time of Nicky's retirement from the Matildas, she was a playing assistant coach in the Women's National Soccer League (WNSL) known as the Ansett Summer Series, which was established in 1996.

I was also playing at South Melbourne, and I played futsal for both Victoria and the national team 1990–1993. I went to Brazil in the futsal national team in late 1993, and we also played the Brazilians in Sydney in July 1993—this was under my married name, Azzato.

From South Melbourne Nicky moved to Brunswick Zebras, playing 1995–1997/8.

> In 1996, I broke my leg in the Division 1 grand final. This was one week before the Open National Champs in Darwin. I was the state team forward, and I crashed into the goalkeeper on the other team – who happened to be the state team keeper. She ended up with concussion, and I broke my leg. We both missed out on going to Darwin and the national champs, which would have been my seven years representing for Victoria. Therefore, I think I started my state team journey in 1990 and finished in 1997.

In 1998, Nicky retired from the game for several years.

> It was in the lead-up to the Sydney 2000 Olympics. Victoria had an ITC program, and I was coaching with Jeff Olver—who ultimately became my partner. The fact that we had met through soccer and had developed a relationship was tricky as we were both working in football.
>
> He was the Victorian state coach in 1994, which is the year Victoria hosted the national championships. The Victorian senior team finished runners-up to NSW. Jeff was also the U/19s coach in 1996 and 1997 and during that time was also the Victorian ITC coach—I was the assistant coach. Jeff was also involved in the women's national team with Tom Sermanni, and both he and Greg Brown were joint national coaches in 1997, when Tom Sermanni took a job somewhere else.
>
> Soccer was very political, and ultimately Greg Brown got the national team job over Jeff and then left under questionable circumstances. That meant the women's national team went into the Sydney 2000 Olympics with a lot of baggage and quite a few coach changes in the lead-up. Subsequently, they didn't too well.

In 1999, the VWSA amalgamated with Football Federation Victoria in the lead-up to the 2000 Sydney Olympic Games. Many opposed the move, not wanting the men's federation to take over all they had worked so hard to achieve.

> It was a significant change when the VWSA came under the umbrella of the men—there's good and bad in that. The good is that it grew; you've got lots of junior development, and you've got more money coming into the game. The bad is you've lost that individualised kind of service and, having said all that, there were many passionate advocates as part of the men's

> association who really wanted to see the women's game grow and develop. The unfortunate part of that is perhaps some of those initial competitions and those pioneers who paved the way have kind of got lost a little bit with it only growing under the men's umbrella, when that's not really true. You know there was a very strong vibrant competition and lots of really good things happening in women's games prior to it being associated with the men.
>
> I retired from playing and I coached for a while. I coached at a good level and like, I have the equivalent of the B Licence, in the modern terminology, and I coached the elite boys for a long time. I did development squads and state teams. I was involved with the women's game for a bit, but I just got really burnt out and I got sick of politics, and I just happily walked away from the game. I had a break from the game completely for probably seven or eight years.

Nicky exited retirement to play alongside friends in the World Masters Games in 2002, where they were beaten in the final. After tasting success, they entered a team in the Sydney Games.

> Then we got back involved with the World Masters about eight years ago, and a few of the people you've interviewed, we all got together, and we played in Melbourne and we won a silver medal. And again, I had a break, I didn't do anything, and then we were really keen to play in the Sydney World Masters. We got a team together that was across Australia. We called ourselves Random United because we randomly gathered all these players. We won a gold medal, and I had such a great time and I went, 'Oh, I want to go back to playing.'

So Nicky did. In her 40s, she played three seasons with the Darebin Falcons.

> I started back in Division 2 and, ironically, I'm finishing in Division 2 locally, with the Darebin Soccer Club. They didn't have a coach this year so I've kind of coached and played this year. It was fun, but my body couldn't put up with the rigours of football and injury forced me into permanent retirement.

Like many other players in this book, Nicky recalls how much dedication and sacrifice elite play required. But despite the hard work, and success, women got little financial support.

(A woman's) got to make a choice ... she starts to think about having children and cement(ing) her marriage, and she's got to give her career up to do that, where a bloke can, you know, biologically, just continue to play and still be a dad. So you know, there are lots of things that you've got to weigh up as a female that impacts incredibly on your elite athlete status.

I must admit, when you play at the highest level, you're incredibly dedicated. But there's not the funding that's around today; there's not the exposure that there is today. I mean we often say that you (could) have bought and sold a house in what it cost us in leave without pay. The Australian Indoor Team used to tour Brazil or South American countries, and that was a $2,000, $3,000 or $4,000 trip. It was $500 to go for a week at the AIS, and you had to pay for your gear.

I mean, my first tournament we didn't even have gear, and here I am five foot tall. I was given a man's basketball tracksuit for Australia—from a six foot four inch bloke, and I'm trying to wear this tracksuit! Look, I'm five foot, and I had to roll it right up.

So, it's really great to have seen the changes in the game and recognition for the girls. And I guess we helped pave the way, but look, I was only ever on the fringes. I mean, I kind of got into the Australian team really when there wasn't a lot happening, and I was really retiring and moving to coaching when there was an injection of tournaments and development and the whole ... exposure.

Reflecting on her coaching career, Nicky notices the game is changing—and for the better. Women coaches are slowly gaining respect, and young girls are playing in school teams.

In 1996/7, I was working for the FFV, or the VSF as they were then ... as a sports development officer, and I was doing soccer clinics in schools. Now, what I really noticed in a short period of time was when I first started doing that, I'd go into a school and all the boys would go, 'But you're a girl. Girls don't play soccer,' and, 'What would you know?' and, you know, 'Girls don't play that.' And you'd do a few tricks and by the time you'd finish they'd be like, 'Oh, okay.'

Now across a two-year period, which I think is when the junior girls league was starting to get off the ground, there was a lot more exposure about girls playing soccer. I probably did that job for three or four years, and when I finished, I'd go into a school and there was absolutely no comment about the fact that I was female. Most of the primary schools had a girls' team, and the boys just accepted that girls played soccer.

That was the most significant change, and I guess the other thing was when I was at high school, I used to wag PE in that the girls had to do dancing and the boys got to do football and soccer. So, I actually was given a bad mark in PE cause I used to wag the girls' dancing and go and play football and soccer with the boys. And because I could play, the PE teacher let me do that. But then they wouldn't grade me on that, so that was again because girls weren't seen to be, you know, (in) any of the ball sports, and I can't dance. I've got two left feet. You know, I'm good with my left foot on the soccer field but not on the dance floor!

Nicky also remembers how her relationship impacted her career.

There's always politics in sport, and I ended up in a personal relationship with someone who was working in women's football as well, and that caused a lot of distress for lots of different reasons. He was a high-profile coach, and I was a player, and we did a lot of development work together and, where we felt we were very professional, that caused a lot of angst and a lot of politics in the soccer community.

That made it really difficult, and in the end, it really affected our relationship. We probably went our separate ways because of the politics, and I was completely fed up with all the bureaucratic stuff, and I walked away from the game without a backward glance for at least 10 years. So it really had an impact on my life in lots of different ways, and it took a long time to repair that.

And again, it's just people. Soccer is a game of opinions, and everyone is entitled to their opinion. But sometimes when that impacts on you personally, that really burns you in regard to the game. And I also found being a woman in a men's environment—so when I was coaching elite boys' teams—that men were intimidated by the fact that I was well qualified, and I knew what I was doing and that I had ... I always had my players' respect from the boys, but not sometimes their parents. And culturally, I had a stint at the Melbourne Knights Football Club, and they were very confronted by a female in a male role—and a good female who took their elite team to a good result and it was a dreadful experience.

I went overseas in late 1998, and when I returned in 1999, I started coaching boys. I did a number of Centre of Excellence squads (1998/9/2000), and then

I coached the U/14 boys development squad—Victoria beat NSW in the final in 2001 at the Friendship Games. I also coached U/16 boys at both Brunswick City Soccer Club in 2000 and Melbourne Knights in 2001. I also coached the Victorian women's state teams during this time: U/16 girls for two years and U/19 girls for two years—this was while I was still playing state myself.

But again, I got to a point where I went look, I have confidence in my ability, I feel I can compete with any man. The men are intimidated by that. I had a number of run-ins with male coaches who tried to bully me and stand over and intimidate me because I was a woman, and really you just go, guys, like we should just work alongside each other. But I certainly found that (in that) era, and it's probably changed significantly now because that was probably 10 or 15 years ago. As a person paving the way for women coaches in a male-dominated environment, that certainly was taxing, and I was very happy to walk away and not be involved in any capacity for a long time. And I still find there are some men who are intimidated by me as a woman because I can hold my own in a soccer conversation. You know, you learn a lot along the way.

There (are) a few new people who know females who are involved in the game at elite level, and there is a pathway now for retiring Matildas to get involved in coaching. I'd have welcomed that with open arms, but unfortunately that wasn't around when I was retiring and becoming a coach. I had to pay, and I think what's unfortunate these days, it's great that they've got the licensing, but to progress my licence, it's going to cost me about $15,000. There's no incentive for me to pay that money because I can't coach at a high level, and unless I'm coaching at an elite level, I can't afford to pay $15,000 and take six or seven weeks off work to be upgraded and to go to the workshops. And so it's a catch-22.

I'm really restricted in that and look, that would be also for male coaches, but there are more job opportunities for men than women, and that's the most senior pathway in the country. So if anything could change in women's football, that would be something, you know, that incentive and that pathway progression for female coaches would be it.

I mean you need an A Licence to coach at A-League level. You need a B Licence to coach at the W-League level or an undertaking to get to that, an undertaking to do your B Licence, so the women coaches in the W-League would be in that process. That's quite an expensive process as it is, and I don't quite have all the units in my B Licence and again because I had that 10-year time out, I had to do a whole series of upgrades along the way. Because I've

> kind of got back into coaching this year with my, you know, social team, I've sort of looked into that a little bit and it's just cost prohibitive. So while I'd love to be able to maintain my accreditation, financially and realistically it's just not worth it.
>
> And I can't get a job at the right level to help me pay for it. My husband is doing the same thing. He's a highly qualified male coach who has to pay $12,000 to get his A Licence, and again we're wrestling with—is there a reason to do that? So if both of us did it that's $24,000, you know—we're just not going to do it. Why would you do it?

As to the future of women's coaching in Australia and the professional side of football in Australia:

> I mean look, I'd love to (see) a female coach an A-League team because really, a female could coach an A-League team. But community perception would never accept that, and they would never even give them, I don't believe, an opportunity even in an assistant role. When I was involved, I did kind of challenge the system, and I certainly tried to get an under-21 job at a men's club in the pathway. I was very well qualified and easily could have done the job, but because I am a female I certainly wasn't given the opportunity, and that's unfortunate. I think that is still what happens in the game, and you know, men are accepted as coaches in women's sport yet women aren't accepted as coaches in men's sport. So from that perspective, I think they're treated very much as second-class citizens.

Nicky expresses indebtedness to the people she has met during her career and is pleased with her achievements. Through her husband's football academy, she is still involved with the game today.

> I divorced my first husband because of soccer influences, and then I met my partner, who became my husband the second time around. So soccer's had an incredible impact on my life—good and bad. And look, he's a former Socceroo, he's an Olympian, he's done amazing things. It's nice to be able to stand beside him and go, you know, I do some of those things too. I think that's really satisfying.
>
> You don't take notice of those things while you're playing because you just, you set goals you want, you know, you never think you're going to get picked

in the state team, and you do, and then you go I never thought we'd win a state tournament and we did, and then you go, 'And oh my god, I scored the winning goal in that game,' and no one can ever take that off you. And while it is significant and great fun at the time, it's only when you retire and you look back and go, 'Oh, my resume's not too (bad), you know, that's okay.'

And then I loved coaching. I really challenged myself in the male environment and I deliberately wanted to test myself against the men. While I may not have got recognition for that, personal satisfaction I went, 'Yeah, I can, I did my qualification with Ange Postecoglou. So you know, you look at the level that Ange is coaching now and I go, you know what, I can coach like he can, and I could still coach like he can except he's a man and he's got a pathway and a job opportunity, and I'm a woman and I don't.'

And look, if I really, really wanted it, I probably could have got back involved in a national team. But it's so time consuming, and it's a lifestyle and I went, personally, I feel I could stand up against an Ange and I don't need to challenge myself anymore. I've done that, so I think personal satisfaction, and I've also met some incredible people, obviously my current partner, my husband. I've been to countries and done things that you never thought possible, so it's one of those things—like I did a volunteer project around soccer in New Guinea as part of the peace process so, you know, without soccer, I wouldn't have had any of those experiences, so it's terrific really.

Nicky is a staunch advocate for the recognition of the pioneers of the women's game in Australia and strongly believes that they should be acknowledged for their dedication.

I'd also really like, you know, those champions to have some recognition: people like Carolyn Monk, like Jane Oakley, Debbie Nicholls, Jeanette Melvyn, Tracey Hodge. There's a whole lot of people who really dedicated their lives and careers to women's football and the development of women's football. But because they're no longer necessarily involved and there's not been that documented history, that stuff has kind of got lost. And that's really unfortunate because I think there's been, you know, they championed the cause. They helped make it what it is today. Look, the men talk about it as well. My husband is a former Socceroo; (he) acknowledges that they all paved the way for the next team. You know the Socceroos have got their own damn plane, you know. I'm sure the girls would like their own plane.

Each generation before says they pave the way, but I think what the men's game does fairly well is they had that recognition, and the women's game is just starting to catch up from that perspective. So if nothing else, I guess that's what I'd like to champion as best we can is that those founders and those people who went before, whether it's at elite level or just that club administrator, that supported that team all the way through over a long period of time, that there was recognition for that. That'd be significant.

I think without the Maggies, the Bettys, the Theresas—you lose that history. I have sitting in my cupboard a whole photographic history of the ITC and the Ansett Summer Series. But where do I take that, and who do I give that to, that I can trust to hold that information and to be honest. The FFV ... haven't had the capacity or the space or even the interest to want to do that, and that's a bit sad, I think.

Nicky is still involved in football today, empowering young girls and women to become the sport's future.

Jeff and I are together and married these days. He is still heavily involved in football, so I still have some involvement through him. He runs his own goalkeeping academy—Jeff Olver Football Zone Coaching—so I assist with that and do most of our marketing and stuff. It's fun. I don't coach anymore, but occasionally I will do school talks and speak with kids at school about women in football.

I am very pleased to finally see some equity in the pay for female footballers alongside their male counterparts. It's long overdue, but how we wish pay was even an option for our day. I had to pay to go to the AIS, and I certainly had to fundraise to play overseas. There was no free gear, social media or even acknowledgement really back in our day. So it's a lovely change to see the profile and media cover of women's football today.

15. Paul Turner

*They should play, let them play,
encourage them to play.*

Paul Turner is the only male pioneer included in this book (outside of the references to the valued contributions of Arthur Watson, Mick and Jason Hoar, Callan McMillan and Paul Hughes).

Paul was appointed as the National Executive Director of AWSA during the watershed years of the 1990s and was involved the administration of Australian women's football during a time of great change. While Paul was only to spend a short time with the women's association he was witness to and part of a period which included two World Cups (1995 and 1999), the Sydney Olympics in 2000 and the amalgamation of AWSA with the ASF.

Paul Turner became National Executive Director of the AWSA in 1993, the third in the role after Keith Gilmour and Heather Reid. Paul came from Western Australia to play football with the AIS and worked with the both the ACT Soccer Federation and the ACT Touch Association before returning to WA to work as a schoolteacher. He returned to Canberra soon after to be the NED of the AWSA. I caught up with Paul on 19 July 2012 to chat about his role in the development of women's football during his short time with the AWSA during the tumultuous 1990s.

The 1990s heralded a new era for women's football in Australia. After FIFA's trial Women's World Cup tournament in 1988, the official inaugural tournament was scheduled for 1991 in China. Then the International Olympic Committee (IOC) announced they would include women's football in all future Olympic Games in 1993, and two years later saw a second World Cup in Sweden, swiftly followed by the Olympic Games in Atlanta in 1996 and the build-up to the Sydney Olympics in 2000. It was a whirlwind of high-profile events, during which the administration of the game was also undergoing major upheaval, with the AWSA debating coming under the jurisdiction of the ASF. And in 1995, the women's national team gained their moniker of the 'Matildas' after a competition was run by local radio station SBS.

But Paul's first encounter with women's football and the issues they faced came far earlier than the 1990s.

> My first experience of women's football, look, I didn't know they played. When I was playing, it wasn't encouraged, and the odd girl would play, and she'd play generally in a boys' team and then she'd get to 13 or 14 and basically be told she couldn't play.
>
> I can remember, my father got into a little bit of a to-do with one of the girls, a girl's father, when we lived in a country town about exactly that. He basically was the coach of the team, and the girl was whatever age, and he sort of said, 'It's probably about time she goes somewhere else.' I don't know if there was anywhere else for her to go, I think back now. At the time, I didn't have any idea, but they had a bit of a heated discussion about it because the dad said she's capable and confident, and look, she was capable and confident enough to play. But you know how it was.

When Paul entered women's football officially, Australia was still getting to grips with failing to qualify for the inaugural Women's World Cup. Indeed, the country was one of the most vocal in convincing FIFA to instigate the tournament, so their knockout was a heavy blow. But the Matildas pressed on, trying to qualify for the second World Cup.

> At that time, I'd done a bit of playing, coaching, and as I say, the opportunity then arose to get involved and I applied for the job (of NED). It was, I guess, an interesting couple of years ... At that stage, the women's association was separate to the ASF. They had their separate entity, separate positions, and were trying to do some separate activities, although many of their core activities were still done by the ASF or the state federation, the state men's federation.

The AWSA had moved to the capital city in 1986 to take advantage of an improving relationship with the Australian Sports Commission (ASC). The new base for the AWSA secretariat opened on February 27 that year in the ACT Sports House in Hackett, a suburb of Canberra.

> I was the NED, so I came in as the, in effect I guess, the CEO, reporting to a board of management, a voluntary board that was selected or elected by the

states. I came in and, look, at that stage, it was very early in the piece. We had, what, when I moved in, one, 1.5 people in the office, with me being the full-time person and a half-time receptionist/secretary. We did actually have a development officer for a one-year appointment who was finishing as I sort of arrived. So, before me I guess, they had 2.5 people, but one of them was only on a 12-month government grant to do some development work. And by the time I left, we were up to I think it was five full-time staff.

Paul managed the organisation's communication and administration. However, because of the upheavals in the game and the workload required to support a national team trying to qualify for several international tournaments during the 1990s (three World Cups and an Olympic Games), things began to change.

The AWSA's major requirement was actually to do the administration and get stuff out to states, that sort of thing, more so than, say, policy or direction. Although the problem was, the board was sort of looking at that as a key requirement, so on one hand, you had states saying, 'We just want information, tell us what's going on.' And the board was then saying, 'Hey, we want a marketing plan, or a strategic plan going forward.' And you know, well, okay, which one is it going to be? Or to try to do both with 1.5 people is quite difficult.

Then on September 20, 1993, the OIC announced the addition of women's football as a full medal event at the Atlanta Olympic Games in 1996. Four days later, it announced Sydney as the host city of the 2000 Olympic Games.

Sydney got the Olympics, which meant that we automatically qualified. And what they put in place from the Australian Olympic Committee was what they called their Gold Medal Plan. So we were responsible for, I guess, implementing that plan right from the start, and also the national team were entering their second Women's World Cup ... You then had this dilemma of, on the one hand, states saying, 'We want communication, and we want the general administration stuff—send us our stuff.' And on the other hand, we needed to get a seven-year plan to try and get into the gold medal position at the Sydney 2000 Olympics, which we didn't get but that was the plan.

We went from being an organisation that was turning over probably a quarter of a million dollars, of which $150,000 of that was probably coming from government, to turning over about $1.1 million in the space of 12 months, of which probably $1m of that was from government.

The Gold Medal Plan also created its own issues. In 1993, the AWSA was still an independent body, and the men's organisation had little interest in the women's game. But after the gold medal funding was announced, Soccer Australia was unimpressed. McGowan and Crawford state that Soccer Australia made numerous attempts to bring the women's game under its control after the funding announcement. The AWSA refused them all.

> (It was) because we were allowed to put our own submission forward and so was obviously the Australian Soccer Federation, so it wasn't a joint submission. It was just the Australian Soccer Federation put in a submission for the men's team, Australian Women's Soccer Federation put in a submission for the women's team, and we were separate for the initial submissions.
>
> As it evolved, they merged the requirements, I think, leading up to Sydney a couple of years out. But it meant we got a million bucks or thereabouts, bit over, and so did the Australian Soccer Federation—which they weren't happy about because basically we got an equal amount and they thought they should, one, have been putting in the submission and, two, have probably gotten more for the men's team than the women's team. Again, we were very small in comparison, was their argument.

Paul believes one of the biggest issues for the women's game is how Football Australia's operating model focuses too heavily on the men's game.

> That's the problem, and I think that was always the problem ... Women's football's not really our core business. Our core business is getting the men's team to qualify for a World Cup, and I think that still is the case. In fact, other programs and other things sometimes suffer through the fact that they see that as being their core business. So, I think the A-League suffered because they were trying to win a World Cup ... I think the junior youth teams have suffered because their core business has been trying to get their ... senior men's team to the World Cup.

Rather battling the ASF, Paul found conflict often came from within the AWSA. While he acknowledged the reasons for the AWSA's strong self-belief and desire to remain autonomous, he thought that the organisation would be better off under the umbrella of the ASF. This ruffled some feathers within the women's association.

> I guess one thing it did create within the ranks of the women's associations, both state and national itself, was whether I was an Australian Soccer Federation plant or person rather than acting on behalf of the Australian Women's Soccer Association.
> ... I wasn't as well received within my own organisation. So I think I was very well received outside, within the Australian Soccer Federation side of things and the state federations, but there was probably a little bit of, I don't know whether it was concern or, you know, a little bit of. 'Is this guy just working for us or working for them?'
> Now, I guess that was sort of part of the era and the period. The reason they've made a separate women's association was because of obviously feeling that they were neglected and isolated in some of the decisions and, you know, the opportunities and so on.
> My view was that rather than fight and separate, you know, at the end of the day the Australian Soccer Federation was the FIFA member. So if we wanted to participate in the World Cup, we had to go through the Australian Soccer Federation to enter us into that competition. It was probably much easier to enter with their support than enter with, you know, fighting at the time. So I didn't even feel like it was a problem outside—it was probably my own personal point of view, more a problem inside when I got in there and being involved from within. People sort of looking at me a little sceptically or different or whatever or (are) not sure whether I was the most appropriate person.

Problems within the AWSA continued over the use of the funding and the appointment of a national coach leading up to the Olympic Games.

> That circumstance actually brought a clash between Board members and myself because I was of the view that we had a million bucks, we could put $100,000 or thereabouts into buying a coach, a darn good coach. (But) we had Board members who were saying, 'Why would we want to? We haven't got enough for a coach to do a full-time job, and why would we want one anyway?'
> So, we could get a part-time coach, but they weren't interested in getting a full-time coach. We also then had circumstances where the states could then

start to put in their academies and buy coaches, so we then had situations where again we were looking for the best person we could get, and whether that someone would come from coaching boys and was now wanting to shift across and coach girls' or women's teams because they were now getting paid for it, as in paid as a proper job, and that created a few tensions within the state people as well.

Paul's views on appointing a national coach created further argument. Some members found his views on the selection process discriminatory and unsupportive of women in coaching roles.

You know, you're getting people who said, 'Yet again you're getting the boys' coaches in, whereas all our women's coaches have been around for years doing the jobs and whatever for nothing, and now you're moving them out.' Now our argument there was, you've got a coach who's been coaching at the highest level you know, say coaching a national league team or coaching youth teams or whatever and they put their hand up for the job, you'd surely want to at least talk to them. I would have thought—again, some people thought not. So I guess there were more tensions; the tensions I found were within rather than out(side).

To give you an example, we had the national team playing against Russia on the Gold Coast, and we picked two teams: a green and gold A and B teams, and the B team didn't have a coach. So, we had a lady who was a level 3 coach, played for Australia, married to a director of coaching up there but, you know, had done all the coaching badges, was coaching up there at a good level in their academy program. So we said, 'Do you want to be involved in coaching the team?' I thought that was a darn fine idea and, you know, an appropriate move because I didn't know how good a coach or not she was, but she had all—she ticked all the relevant boxes, and we were struggling. We were in dire straits because the coach had pulled out a week to 10 days before we were due to start.

I very quickly got notified by the Board that that was an inappropriate procedure in selection, and she wasn't an appropriate appointment anyway to have made. So not only was it an inappropriate process, it was an inappropriate appointment. And I could not for the life of me understand why it was an inappropriate appointment given that I had looked at it, she ticked every single box, and you would have said being proactive to support a woman.

> Here she was, she wasn't the right woman. So, we had a lot of women on the Board saying that she's not the appropriate woman. So, I actually found that sometimes women were the stumbling block on women.
>
> Now, for what reason—there could have an enormous number of reasons. I don't know the extent of all those reasons. I don't know what she had or hadn't done, or what her past represented or didn't represent to some of these other people. You know, that's the sort of example of, I guess, conflict that you talk of. It seemed to be a no-brainer to me but obviously someone thought I had no brains. (Laughter.) Instead of being a no-brainer, I had no brain.

Ultimately, despite the conflict, Paul agreed all involved were in it for the right reasons and had the best intentions.

> Look, there (were times) in the boardroom when I'd say, 'It's black,' and people would say, 'No, it's white.' And we had some stand-up battles about what should or shouldn't—or the way it should be done.
>
> At the end of the day, I think we all wanted to see the game move forward. I just think there was, there were issues with how I either wanted to do it or how I was seen to want to do it, and how they wanted to do it or how I saw them wanting to do it. And it just meant we created, I guess, a conflict situation.
>
> The reality is, everyone's heart was in the right place to try and move the thing forward. It's just that we had some different perspectives and different ideas and different views. I thought it could go much more quickly or easily or smoothly or in a better way, and other people had their own thoughts.

Paul left the AWSA in 1995 to take up an academic job in Melbourne but stayed involved in the game. He joined the VWSA board in 1996 through to 1999 and, during the same period, was elected to the AWSA board in 1997/98.

> And then when my kids got involved, the girls got involved—I started doing a bit of coaching in the girls' games as well. I stayed involved in the Boards up until about 1998/99, somewhere around there, and then probably drifted away until about 2005–2006 when my eldest daughter started to sort of get involved again. And I just started watching, thinking, you know, watching what the coaches were doing and thinking, well, yeah, I can still do that. I can still see that, so I thought I'd get back involved, so that's what I've done since.

So Paul's involvement in the women's game came full circle: when I interviewed him, he was coaching his eldest daughter's team, and he undertook several coaching and managing roles for his three daughters up until 2016. He reflected on how his perspective changed as a father, regarding the struggles women and girls in the sport face.

> I reckon it's a great game for girls and women. I don't necessarily mean women should play with men, but certainly, you know, it's a good game for women to play. My girls have enjoyed their time being involved. My middle daughter played in a boys' team, and she was the only girl for a number of years. She had no problems with doing that.
>
> My eldest one started off and was one girl in a small-sided football … competition. She dropped out 'cause she didn't like being the only girl. So, it was only a couple of years later, so she would have been about 10 or 11 when she started, and she dropped out for a couple of years and then when she was about 12, she said, 'Can I start playing again, but I want to play in a girls' team?'
>
> We found a girls' team, an all-girls' team for her. Although she quite enjoys playing against the boys, she just doesn't want to play in a boys' team. And my littlest one, she started. She played in a small-sided football comp and was the only girl again and just said, 'I don't want to be the only girl.' So if she had have had another girl, she would have kept coming, so I've lost her to netball now.
>
> I'm now coaching a Metro Division women's team. The Metro Division senior women's, but my 15-year-old, middle daughter, is involved in that one. Yeah, I'm enjoying it.

However, Paul's introduction to coaching a women's team went awry. He experienced first-hand what can happen when a club is not fully supportive of women in football.

> My very first step back in the water was with the women's team in the State League 1, which is below the Premier League. Then we managed to survive relegations. I'd thought we'd done pretty well, but the Board obviously didn't. They just said, 'See you later,' as they do. And as it turns out, look, we'd set up a system in place where we thought we could actually move on; they had different ideas.

And, unfortunately, a lot of the girls left the team and dropped from State One to State Two, then last year to State Three, you know, which is a bit sad, and they lost a lot of their good players. That's not to say that I would have retained them or anything else. It's just unfortunate that the circumstances they put themselves in, or put the girls in, you know. They had a coach and then basically said, 'No, we'll test the market and see if we can get anyone else, and the reality was they got no one.'

Then by that stage they'd lost the coach, so they then had to go and find someone who could fill in. You know, it's not really the best way of doing things. But that's club land, we all live with it.

While we were discussing coaching generally, Paul reflected on how far the women's game had progressed since he first started coaching in Canberra. He had the opportunity to test his state boys' team against the Matildas under coach Fred Robbins, who took up the role in 1985 and is recognised today by FFA as coach of the 1979–89 women's team of the decade.

I was coaching an ACT under-13s state side, and we played the senior women's national team—the actual, you know, the Matildas—and we smacked them about five or six nil. I will always remember the coach Fred Robbins saying something like, 'Your boys are just too rough.'

... I always remember that when I went and got the job (as NED), the difference in quality in that sort of 15-year period was just enormous. I looked and thought, my 13-year-old boys would not have been able to beat the 1992 women's side. And I tell you what, if they played them now, I reckon it would be about a 7, 8, 10, 12-nil smacking the other way at least—probably more. And probably, if the ACT boys played the Matildas, you know, it would a cricket score the other way, so you know, that's a huge advancement and pretty quickly, too, which was impressive, you know.

At AWSA, Paul witnessed many of the major moments in the history of the women's game. These include qualifying for the 1995 Women's World Cup in Sweden, working towards the Sydney Olympics in 2000, and developing the new Women's National Soccer League (WNSL), which began in 1996/97.

I feel comfortable enough saying that I left the game or women's side of the game in a better state, that is, to say that it had gone forward. Then the people who came after me left it in a better position, and so on. You know, things like the time we initiated the very first national league setup. I wasn't in the position to actually make it happen, but we put in place the foundations for it to actually come about. The person who came in after me was the one who actually made the thing work. I then missed attending the World Cup in 1995 because I'd left the job by then, so again that's probably something I would have liked to have been involved in.

During the 2000 Sydney Olympic Games, Paul was the Competition Coordinator for Melbourne Football for the Sydney Olympic Broadcasting Organisation (SOBO). He was also a recipient of the Australian Sports Medal in 2000. Overall, he is proud of the women's game.

You've got the women's team, senior team, who have won an international trophy before your men have even got close to one, and they're going to win a World Cup long before the men ever get close to winning one.

Paul is still living in Melbourne and is currently a senior lecturer with Deakin University. He is no longer involved with football other than catching up socially with friends he made working for women's football during the turbulent years of the 1990s in Australia. 'It was, I guess, an interesting couple of years,' he said.

16. Louisa Bisby

You gain respect with your feet.

Louisa Bisby is a success story in women's football in Australia. Louisa migrated to Australia in 1995, and had two games with the Matildas between 1999 and 2007 (one A international), and played in the W-League. After retiring from playing in 2012 due to injury, Louisa worked with Melbourne Heart FC to promote the virtues of the game to the wider community including ethnic and less privileged groups. She is mentor to young women footballers and is still involved today with Melbourne Heart's successor, Melbourne City FC.

Born in Royal Leamington Spa, England, in 1979, Louisa Bisby kicked her first football for an Australian team at 15—the year her family immigrated.

> Growing up in England, I naturally grew up watching and playing the sport, so I think it was just in the blood. There are plenty of photos of me as a child with a ball, whether it be a tennis ball, soccer ball at my feet or in my hand. I always remember playing at primary school, in the back garden, kicking the ball against the wall in the park by myself or with the lads from the local estate. The boys would just come along and ask to join in. It is just something that naturally came to me, and my dad encouraged me to play.

Louisa played her first game of football for her local school in England. The times required young girls play in boys' teams, though the authorities soon barred this.

> My first team was a primary school team at Brookhurst Primary School. I had my hair cut short like a boy when I was five or six so I could participate in the school's competition. I was always playing football in the playground with a tennis ball and if it wasn't with a tennis ball, then it was a mini-football or a normal-sized football on the grass fields.

It was common for young talented girls to play for senior women's teams during this period; Louisa was no exception.

> Football began with the school team, which then led into school holiday programs and clinics such as Coventry City and Aston Villa, which is where I got spotted and asked to play for my first senior football club outside of school. I was 12 years old, and Coventry City wanted me to be a mascot, and Aston Villa said I could play. So I chose Aston Villa to be my first official competition team at a senior level. Unfortunately, I broke my leg in that first year. So I played one year, broke my leg and, from memory, there was another season before leaving for Australia.

Louisa, her sister and father arrived in Melbourne on January 15, 1995. 'Mum and Dad divorced when I was one, so Dad brought my twin sister and I up since then.' Louisa's father encouraged his daughters' love of sport.

> I was always playing sport. It didn't matter what, whether it was tennis, running or basketball, skateboarding—anything as long it was outdoors, and it didn't matter if I was good or not. It was about having fun. If there was any opportunity for me to be outside playing, it was just a natural environment to me. I was very earthy. If it rained, I would put on my wellington boots and go and jump in the puddles.
>
> Our dad encouraged both my sister and I to do anything we wanted to do—no questions asked, just go and do it. He was probably the biggest influence. If he didn't say go play sport or keep up with it, then I wouldn't be playing.
>
> Just being outside every day, they are the biggest memories that I have— running around every minute of the day. It didn't matter if I was at school, inside doing my homework, I had a football at my feet. I would be in the park playing football with the boys until it was pitch-black. We would go down to the dairy and kick a ball. No matter what ... we always had a football close by. It was just lots of fun.

The women's game was growing rapidly, with Victoria home to over 20 senior women's teams in 1990. This increased to 65 senior teams and seven U/17 teams by 1998. The AWSA also announced the Women's National Soccer League (WNSL) Ansett Summer Series in 1996. This replaced the annual state and territory tournaments, which had been operating for 23 years and had provided the base for selection into the national team.

Louisa began playing in Australia with the Doncaster Rovers. But her career included stints with Brunswick Zebras SC, Manningham United SC, Moorabbin Soccer SC, Ringwood City SC and Box Hill United SC, and she was with Bundoora United in 2012. Tom Sermanni, Australian national coach, soon spotted her talent and began to include her in national training camps. So started Louisa's international career.

> Whilst it was my first year playing football in Australia at Doncaster Rovers SC, I got asked to represent the Victorian U/16s, U/19s and seniors state teams. From this, I got asked to be a member of the ITC program (now known as NTC) and played in the Women's National League.

Then in 2002, Mike Mulvey, the coach of the under-19s Australian women's team for the World Cup, came to Louisa with a proposition.

> He knew that I wasn't going to be part of the Australian team, so he asked if I would like to go to gain more experience. It was during the World Cup in 2002 when I played in the Chinese Super League for Schaun, Chengdu in central China.

Louisa returned to Australia and played with Box Hill for three years, winning the WPL Gold Medal in 2003. The next year she again travelled overseas to play professionally in the German Bundesliga for FFC Brauweiler Pulheim (now FC Koln).

> Both the clubs I played for in China and Germany were of the same standard as the W-League, if not harder due to both being professional and semi-professional clubs.
>
> In China, the Super League that I played in was for the same duration as the W-League (three months). (It was) short and sharp, but with high-intensity training with at least five to six days of training per week and two times per day. I don't remember having a day off. They had no idea when it came to recovery and rehabilitation. Due to the high-intensity training, I lost 10-15 kgs. Brauweiler FC was a semi-professional club that played all year round, like the Victorian Premier League. The season started in September to June/July/August with a break over Christmas. We trained four nights a week with a game on the weekend.

Her time overseas shaped Louise as both a player and person.

> My strongest memories (are) the experience of living in two foreign countries and appreciating what we have in Australia. It is not so much playing the game but the experience of learning and gaining knowledge about the world, travelling to other countries close by and developing social skills and interpersonal skills that helped me learn to communicate with people from all different races, social backgrounds and personalities. It was great to meet foreigners and bring a bit of Australia internationally as a senior player. The experience (showed me) how I could help guide other people in a positive manner and how young players can teach you a lot about yourself as a person, your faults, your strengths and your weaknesses.

The support of family and friends is paramount to the ongoing participation of women in football.

> We only saw (my mother) every fortnight growing up, so she knew about my football. But because she had never seen me playing, she didn't really know what football was like.
> It wasn't until she flew over to Germany in 2006/7 and saw me play that she understood the game, why I played and was really proud knowing how I played and also realised how good I was at football. She now looks at football differently and watches the English Premier League, World Cup matches and other international competitions on TV. She is hooked. I would have been very different if I was brought up by my mum, but still would have played a sport. In stating this, she would never have stopped me from playing because she knew how much I loved it.

Louisa's work friends and colleagues also supported her, never questioning her involvement in the game.

> Yes, they were very surprised. Some even Googled me. They would say things like, 'You've got a Wikipedia page!', and in surprise say, 'You play football?' But it is not in a negative way. No matter, they would not let social events hinder my training or games and were never disappointed that I couldn't go away with them during the school holidays because they knew how I loved the sport, and (they) wanted me to succeed … Everyone has always been

supportive. I have never had a family member, friend, teacher or employer tell me to stop playing.

While few women experienced the same, Louisa always felt supported throughout her career and has been fortunate in her relationships with male-dominated clubs and players.

I have not experienced any negativity from male players at an administrative or playing level. I have found that during my career, they have always been very respectful. When a coach respects you as a player and invites you to train with a team, the male players in turn have faith in you because if the coach doesn't trust you then the players won't. In stating this, it is the same within the female game, especially at a national level, (or) when you're a Victorian on a training camp with a number of different girls from the same state. You gain respect with your feet.

I have always been one of three girls that have always trained with a men's team. For example, myself, Selin Kuralay and Melissa Barbieri trained with the boys' team at the VIS under Ernie Merrick during the late '90s. We also trained with South Melbourne SC and Thomas Town SC Youth Team who were coached by Garry Gronewald and Jeff Olver (1974 Australian goalkeeper).

The men will respect you because they will see that you are a good player, and I have never experienced problems to date.

I have not experienced any discomfort/conflict as an administrator, player or coach since I reached a certain age and started puberty. Due to the physical changes, I was unable to play with the boys in the secondary school team. However, that did not deter the lads and I from kicking a ball during break time. By this time, I was old enough to commence playing in a women's team, but I was still able to train and play with the boys in an unofficial way. Having played against young lads and men has helped improved my game.

I have always found that I have been treated respectfully and gained a lot of support—no discrimination in any way.

Louisa's international experiences support her views on discrimination. However, she is mindful of how her fortunate upbringing may not be the same for all women involved in the game.

I experienced no barriers for myself due to being British and having a very open-minded father. For others with different cultural backgrounds and ethnic groups, it maybe a little harder, due to many cultures or families believing females should be more focused on their education or at home.

In China, they treated the women like they would treat men. There was a lot of support. They even brought in an Olympic gold medal long jumper to increase my stamina, agility, speed and reaction times to help me become more mobile on the field. It was a professional environment, and the Chinese wanted to get the best out of me.

The team was treated with the utmost respect and there was no shortage of training gear and football boots given for the season. I also had a very positive experience in Germany and was very well looked after.

It also helped that, as a player, Louisa was fearless.

For myself at the young age of 15/16, I wasn't scared of anyone, but you have to think that other people have a different mentality. Therefore, I ensure that players know I'm a certain person on the field and off the field. I am very competitive on the field and have white line fever!

Louisa again returned to Australia in 2008 and was signed to play for the Melbourne Victory FC, one of the foundation clubs in FFA's then-new national women's football competition, the W-League. At 29, Louisa was selected to play in the club's first game and the season opener against the Central Coast Mariners at the then-named Telstra Dome in Melbourne on October 25, 2008.

While playing in Germany, Louisa realised that progressing her education would assist her future career in football after her playing days were behind her. This led her to the new W-League club Melbourne Heart. Located in the City Football Academy in Bundoora near the La Trobe University, Melbourne Heart FC was founded in 2009 and began playing in the A-League 2010–11 season before being acquired and rebranded as Melbourne City FC in 2014.

I did a Bachelor of Business Sport Leisure Management. So once I graduated from that, I rang up Jeff Miles (then-CEO of Melbourne Victory FC) and asked if any paid positions were available. He said 'No, but why don't you try and contact Melbourne Heart, a new club starting up?'

So I contacted the Melbourne Heart FC Human Resources and emailed my resume. It was(n't) until six months later they rang me up and asked (me) to come for an interview, after obtaining references from Melbourne Heart

FC from Paul Emery (La Trobe University lecturer), Tom Sermanni (Australian national coach) and Amber Beechmore (university placement supervisor from Vicsport).

It just fell in nicely, and this is how I naturally progressed into the administration side of the game. I've been fortunate at a playing level and lucky enough that my career has led me into gaining employment within a sporting organisation. I was quite lucky.

Louisa is full of praise for Melbourne Heart and the opportunity it gave her to promote and assist the development of the women's game. She has also been able to promote the game to a wider multicultural community, providing opportunities to those who might otherwise be sidelined.

While Melbourne Heart FC do not have a W-League team, they are providing the opportunity for young females and aspiring footballers to meet someone that has played at a high level. Regardless (of whether) it is myself or another female employed, it is very positive for the sport.

I am lucky because of the position I am in. I work full time and can help promote the game to the different genders at primary school. It allows boys to see that females can become great players and increases the profile of the women's game. It is very encouraging for young females to have a female role model as once they see a female demonstrate an exercise, they have more self-belief that they can.

Additionally, Melbourne Heart FC conduct free 'Girls with Heart' football clinics, which is about different cultures coming together—Muslims, Jewish, Turkish, Italians, Greeks, Sudanese and Australians coming together to play football. It is helping lift the profile of the women's game and give an opportunity to others who may not otherwise attend a football clinic.

Like all sports, it teaches you how to respect individuals from different cultural backgrounds, ages and experiences of football knowledge. Football teaches you resilience, teamwork, how to be fit and healthy, (to) problem-solve independently and as a group. (It teaches you to) be confident and remain confident when it is not going your way on and off the field. All that you learn whilst playing a team sport and can be brought into the working and family environment.

Football still has its challenges, and Louisa's experience abroad has brought her a unique perspective.

The biggest challenge is providing additional resources and financial support for women in the game due to the low profile of the sport. The only other barriers would be for low-income earners who cannot afford the registration fees and equipment needed, and this doesn't matter if you are a female, male, junior or a senior player.

In China and Germany, clubs get great support from their respective governing body. Overseas and local players do not have to pay their club registration and can gain personal sponsors, accommodation, a car, petrol allowance and insurance. Little things like this make a big difference.

Comparing my personal experience of having played in three different countries, I have always paid my own registration to play in Australia apart from the WLeague level. While in Germany and China, I did not have to pay registration fees, while insurance and accommodation costs were covered.

Support for women who want to raise a family and play football is a common issue, and the lack of childcare support is still a major barrier to participating and continuing in the game. Again, it is the support of family and community that allows women to play.

Another challenge is for females to remain in the sport long term because of the ambition to start or pursue a career which will provide a consistent income or the wish to start a family. However, in stating this, as the years pass, support is slowly growing.

When I was playing for China, it was a full professional set-up. So we would train in the morning, go over to the sports hall and eat, go to sleep in the afternoon, then train again, with the evenings free. We had no responsibility of having to work. You could get your maximum performance, you trained, you could constantly work on your technique and fitness. You had that ability to truly reach your full potential as an athlete and get the maxim out of your body.

In Australia, you don't really get that opportunity. If you want to do that extra training, you would have to get up at six a.m., train hard, go to work and then train again in the evening and then eventually, as you get older, you don't have the same energy as what you would have if you are a high school student where you can get up at seven a.m., do some exercise, then go to school and then come home, have everything ready for you and then go to training. Mum and Dad can drive you everywhere so you can switch off when you are a teenager. But when you are a female adult playing, it is a lot different.

A couple of my friends have had children and they have come back to the game. But you find most of them stop playing because they get another focus, and that is to look after their children. The ones that do come back and play have a supportive husband that wants them to play. That's the difference. Again, it's the family and the community which is the biggest influence on whether a female plays football and continues to play. I have got lots of friends that are in the game because their parents are really supportive. I think that is the biggest thing.

The community has a massive effect. Depending on where you live and which suburb, if they have a football club and have a women's team and females know about that women's team, they are going to go and play for that team. If the club wasn't supportive of females playing sport or football, then females wouldn't play. Or even if they had a boys' team and the coach didn't want the girl to play even though she is better than a few of the boys in the team, then that girl would not get the opportunity to play. The coaches and the community have a massive influence on how a female player would progress.

Louisa retired from playing the game in 2012 due to a knee injury.

I am happy in my job and pretty laid-back, so I don't look too far in the future. I just think about now and what I can do now and how I can help the game grow and how I can help myself grow now as a person rather than in 20 years' time. To think too far in the future, to me that is wasted energy.

Before I left, Louisa imparted a strong call for equality in the game that bears repeating in full:

Because we are female and play a women's sport, does not mean we should have a female coach, referee, lineswoman and administrators. Females should always get the best person for the job regardless of their gender.

17. Jane Natoli

I don't know what it is, but girls just love it, and it's really exciting seeing them getting excited about it.

Like Nicky Leitch and Belinda Wilson, Jane Natoli took a giant step into the male-dominated area of coaching during the 1990s. Jane faced widespread discrimination, intimidation and abuse during those formative years as a female coach and was eventually forced out of the role.

Jane found her feet in the management side of the game and has gone on to play a major role in the development of women's football in the W-League and premier divisions in Victoria.

Jane Natoli was born in Melbourne in 1953 and has been involved in the game as a coach and manager for over 23 years. She is a pioneer in the development of women in coaching and leadership roles in Victoria and at the time of the interview was the team manager for Melbourne Victory in the W-League.

For most who reside in Victoria, AFL is the sport of choice. While football soon stood up to be counted and became a game Jane's daughters could choose, opportunities for women to participate in the game were limited during her youth.

> Growing up with an AFL father, when the kids started playing, we tried getting them into AFL, but they didn't like it. My son moved to hockey anyway—didn't want to compete with his sisters, I don't think. But they love it.
>
> It's funny how they follow it now. My friends joke about it, saying it's such a boring game. It's all AFL down here. One of the other physical education teachers follows Melbourne Victory really closely and follows the women's game. He loves watching them, so we have lots of chats. I would have loved to play it when I was a kid, but it wasn't around and I think back then it would have been a big deal if we were playing football because it was netball and tennis, not soccer.

Like many parents, Jane's children introduced her to football. It was 1997 when Jane, as a mother of two young girls, found herself busy supporting them in roles typically filled by women. However, it was less common for a woman to coach to maintain her children's involvement.

> My kids played every sport when they were little. So it's only been 12, 13, 14 maybe 15 years that I've been involved. I've got twins and they played on the same team, and then Emma played with the boys and got sick of playing with the boys after a couple of years, so I got involved with the club a bit—you know, secretary and the usual stuff females do. A couple of years on the committee and then, because Emma hated playing with the boys, I started coaching the girls, and we formed a girls' team at Croydon Soccer Club.

As the game grew and her daughters began to mature as players, Jane took on the added responsibility of team management duties. And that's how it started.

> So we made a girls' team in the end, and we got a couple more girls (for) a mixture of two teams. And then we had five new teams and then 10 teams in four years. The girls loved it, and then Emma got into the primary school state team (U/12s, run by School Sport Victoria). I was talking to the coach about all sorts of things, and the manager left, and he knew I was a teacher so he said, would I be team manager next year? So after Emma did her stint I became manager, and I was coaching at Croydon and managing there, and that's sort of how it started really.

As her daughters developed, the family left Croydon in search of clubs that could better support their needs.

> We ended up leaving Croydon because, with girls' football, the big problem ... is there's not that many in (players) Victoria ... So the girls that I had—three or four state players in my team at Croydon, and we'd get new girls every year, beginners, absolute beginners coming in at the bottom. So you'd start again teaching them but trying to make it interesting for the other girls.

Jane had never played football; however, her teaching experience and willingness to assist young girls in their pursuit to play was just what the game needed.

> Its only because I'm a physical education teacher that they asked me to coach because I hadn't played before. I played every sport except soccer,

and so we sort of got sick of all those troubles, bringing girls up. I loved it and she loved it, but she wanted to be pushed a bit more so we moved to Ashburton and she played there for a number of years in heading to Premier League. She played, it was in the first 15, reserves and seniors, so she played there until last year and she's now 20. So she played there five or six years, I think. This last year now she's going overseas, and she did have the knee reconstruction—so she hurt her knee in the first game of this season, so she's not playing any more.

My younger one, Alex, just wanted to follow whatever her sister did so she started playing with the under-12s. (She) loved it, so she's followed on and wanted to be in the primary school state team, the same as Emma, and she's got into the state 13, 14 and 15s and then she got into the national squad under-14s and then under-16s, and she's been there for the last three years; she's 16 now.

Alex progressed to play in the W-League with Melbourne Victory and Adelaide United. Jane believes that Alex's success owes much to the improved coaching now offered to women. Previously, this role was filled by well-meaning family members or those not fully invested in developing young girls in football.

Alex received much better coaching than Emma ever did because, by the time Alex started playing, people were starting to be better coaches to the girls. Emma had the same coach for a number of years as a junior after me. I didn't know, you learn by your mistakes. I learnt, but some of the male coaches, they were just there ... I love the way they coach now with the positions, and that would have suited my older one to the tee.

While Jane was happy to coach, her real love was managing.

So I got involved because Emma didn't have a coach. Then the coach of the state team asked me to be his assistant coach for the football federation, so I did that for a couple of years. But I actually prefer managing. I love being with the kids, the girls. I've done boys and girls now, but I like being with the kids, not the pressure of coaching.

For two years I've been the 12-and-under school sport team as coach. I didn't want to do it, but it was sort of pushed on me. I didn't want to coach—I love it, but I don't. I think there are so many more knowledgeable people about football, and I felt—never felt happy because I hadn't played. I'd played high level in other sports but not soccer or football, so I thought I'm better off managing. I know a bit, but I feel there's so many people who can give so much more.

Research on women's involvement in coaching indicates that football, a sport historically associated with men and masculinity, is predominantly occupied by men, even when the participants are female. So the movement of women into leadership and decision-making roles such as coaching is often seen as a significant challenge to the male dominance of the sport. Consequently, the actions of some men in coaching can discriminate against and prevent women from entering. Jane's experience exemplifies the intimidation, inadequacy, abuse, sexual discrimination and marginalisation women can face.

The first coaching course I ever did ... was back in the late '90s. This is my favourite story:
I was with 30 guys, and I think there was one other female, and he was giving out all the tasks for the next day for the assessment. And it was, you know, kicking, goalkeeping, instep pass, trapping. And he looked at me and he went, 'Jane . . . ironing,' and that was, I just went—that was my ... so I thought, 'Nup, never doing another coaching course.' Ironing? Ironing! (Laughter.) Because I was a female in amongst guys and, like, there was hardly a female coach, even though that was only 15 years ago.
Anyway, so about five years later I thought, 'No, I'll do a youth coach's course.' It was supposed to be female-only, and I got there, and there weren't enough females to do it, so there were two of us again, and it was the worst four days I've ever spent. It was just so intimidating with all these males, you know, and people taking the course bowed down to these (men) because they were Premier League players and ... I just hated it. I feel, I'm a teacher and I'm used to talking and instructing. I'm a physical education teacher, but being with all those males, feeling totally out of (my) depth: 'Oh, I'm shit, so it's not worth me doing and I'm terrible at it.' So that's why I don't coach any more—because you have to keep doing courses and I really hate them, and I'm very at home in front of kids (laughter), but not in that situation.

The intimidation and feelings of inadequacy experienced by Jane in the company of men left her feeling marginalised even though she had been coaching for some time:

I've told people since, and no one can believe it and I don't think it would happen now. The coaching courses were terrible. I would fully go to a female one again but never a male one.

The intimidation continued when Jane was the only female responsible for boys' teams. Masculine behaviour traits exhibited by the male coaches—being loud, bullish and bragging—put Jane on edge. This amplified her feelings of inadequacy and lack of confidence while promoting the dominant male and reinforcing the coaching status quo:

> Especially if you're with the boys' team which I was a few times, you're the only female, usually amongst a whole room of males, and that doesn't bother me. We get on well, but I get on well with most people, but it is intimidating especially when a lot of them like to browbeat what I've done, and this is what I've done in the past.
>
> When the boys and I go away with the 12-and-unders, there are three guys and me. It's just the way it is. I'm used to it. But I mean, it is fairly intimidating, especially if you weren't that confident. It's intimidating.
>
> Once I had an issue with and an argument with a coach of the juniors, and he didn't agree. He was playing his best team, and a couple of boys were left on the bench. I was with the girls' team, and I just said something to him that this was a 12-and-under championship not an all-girl championship and the boys, they should all be getting a go. There was a boy in tears on the sidelines, you know, don't you think he should be getting a run? I'm not a confrontational person, but don't you think you should give them some time? He didn't like it.

Jane believes this sexism means women lack the necessary confidence to enter the realms of such a high-powered male domain. Women are more likely to stand back and let the men take the leading role. This reinforces the dominant masculine in coaching and continues to marginalise women, preventing them from feeling they can be competent contributors.

> But that's probably more myself, and I think most females don't want to speak out of turn, tend to be more stand-back-ish and go, 'Well, I'm probably not as good as you, so you do it.' That's what I would think. I think that's probably more a barrier with females. It's more the self confidence that would stop her

saying, 'I'm a good sportsperson, I know I can do it'—to me, that's (what) it was.

Despite the intimidation Jane eventually went back and earned a coaching qualification in futsal.

(It was) just a beginner's one at school, and it was all right. But look, when I go away it's always just me, the only female. You would be hard(-pushed) to find another female, you know, in all the teams scattered around. There's more now, but there's always this big boys' club in all the state teams.

As a result of her experiences, Jane left coaching and concentrated on the management side of the game. By 2012, the W-League was into its fourth season and had returned to its full complement of eight teams after the competition had suffered due to the loss of the Central Coast Mariners in 2010. Jane was the team manager for Melbourne Victory in the W-League for two seasons. In 2012, Melbourne Victory reached their maiden grand final and hosted Canberra United at AAMI Park in Melbourne—only to go down three goals to one. In 2014, the team went one better and recorded the club's first W-League premiership title by defeating Brisbane Roar at Lakeside Stadium two goals to nil.

However, even at the elite level, Jane has witnessed how the women are often treated differently to the men because of their gender and perceived unimportance.

The women Victory squad didn't even get a training uniform last year because the youth boys took it. It disappeared; we never saw it. The girls got a plain tracksuit and a few things and playing gear, and we went trying to find the training gear and it wasn't there, and Adidas said, 'We've sent it out, and you're not getting any more,' so somehow, it's gone to the men. They had no training gear all season. And that's just typical.

The women bore the affront with dignity, but to Jane it still smarted. She notes this type of institutionalised sexism happens at all levels of the game.

Even with my daughter's national team last year, they went to China, and they were supposed to have a training camp in the months coming up to China and they ran out of money after two camps. So the girls met once more before going to China.

That wouldn't have happened if that was a boys' team. They would have found the money. I would guarantee that it wouldn't have happened to a boys' team, they would have funded it somehow and gotten it. So the girls really didn't have the preparation and that showed over the week. Their performance improved and naturally by the end of the week. At the start of the week, they were way out of their depth. So it's sort of accepted that the boys' team get everything and the girls—'yeah, okay, we'll get it later on,' and how they sort the coaches I think often (they say), 'Yeah, okay, it's only the girls, what's left?'

It's just women's football in general. The trouble is, you can moan about it, but women's football doesn't generate sponsorship and doesn't bring crowds so it's very hard to put money and time into women's football when it's not generating any. So I can see why it's as it is; it doesn't make it fair.

I just prefer watching the women, but I think the perception out there is it's women's football and it's rubbish.

Jane also had to contend with her employer's concern over the time she spent managing the state U/12 team in School Sport Victoria. After 10 years in the role as team manager, Jane had to stop due to her employer being unsupportive. The women I interviewed believe it is imperative that women receive support from their workplace if they are to remain involved in the game.

Work doesn't want me to do the managing anymore because with the school sport team I miss a week of school, and they're not happy about that. It wouldn't matter what sport it was, they just don't want me missing school. They don't realise how good it is for the school to have the person out there doing all this, but hopefully I will be able to change their mind by next year. This will be my 10th year, and I want to keep going. And I'm the state convenor for Victoria as well.

Despite the hardships and discrimination, Jane has fond memories of her involvement in the game. 'I'm a bit of a mother to all the girls and kids.'

(I enjoy) being out there and being involved, seeing females involved. I mean just trying to get the girls' teams out there in the local club and trying get as many girls involved at school. The more girls that are involved, the bigger the game becomes.

The experiences of just being away, the drudgery of the week-to-week training, the actual week away is always really special. The way the kids either lift or crumble under the pressure, that's a good experience. It's being with the kids and the relationships you form with them. I still see kids from 10 years ago, and I don't know, to me that's the best reward—except for my own daughter, watching her play and watching my kids play. Apart from that, it's just all good.

There are some really good supporters of the women's game, and I think one of the Melbourne girls from overseas last year stayed with one of the directors of the federation. After watching them and how much they trained and watching a lot more games than he'd watched before, he's turned into a big supporter. I think people just naturally assume that women can't play and don't go and watch. A couple of people from school came and watched a game. I convinced them to come and watch a game last year, and they loved it, so I'd rather watch this than the men's game you know. It will get there eventually, hopefully.

I loved it, it's such a—I know it sounds stupid—it's such a good game for the girls. The kids at school I coach every term at school four days, four teams a week, and once they start playing, they get so enthusiastic. It's something about, I don't know, it's being outside, on the grass, playing a game with boys. I don't know what it is, but girls generally just love it, and it's really exciting seeing them getting excited about it. A lot of kids go and play for clubs after they've done it at school. I don't know what it is about it—it's just, it's a great game.

Jane is still involved today and is the current team manager for the NPLWFC Bulleen Lions, a women's team in the Premier League in Victoria. She has been in this role for five years—her daughter Alex is now back playing in the league and has joined Jane at the club.

18. Annette Hughes

> *I had a referee say to me once, 'Come on love, this isn't the AFL,' because I was using my body to shield the ball. I'm allowed to use my body, and if it's a 50/50 ball, I'm allowed to challenge for it. I don't have to back off because she looks prettier than me or whatever.*

Annette Hughes came late to women's football in Australia. However, she has played a major role in the development of the game as a player, administrator and mentor to the many young women who are keen to play the game. As a professional woman, Annette was a key player in the changes to how the women's game was administered during the 2000s as a result of the Crawford Report findings.

While Jane Natoli battled the sexism in Australian football as a coach, on the other side of the world, an American named Annette Hughes began playing in the San Francisco Bay Area. It was 1991, and she was 26. Annette's main arena was the Golden Gate Women's Soccer League, northern California's largest football league and part of the California Soccer Association (est. 1902). In the USA, women's football was recreationally focused, not based around individual clubs, with the city running the league. There, women's football had gained popularity during the mid– late twentieth century. But it took the signing into law of Title IX of the 1972 Education Act—which prohibited gender discrimination at institutions such as schools and colleges—for women's participation in football to explode. By the time Annette donned her boots, American women represented 40% of the country's 15 million registered players.

Annette was born in Baltimore, Maryland, in 1965, and was introduced to football by her husband, John, in 1991.

> *I played soccer for the first time when I was 26. At that time, I played softball and tennis and did quite a lot of jogging. I had also run track in high school. I didn't really know much about the game initially, because it wasn't particu-*

larly a popular sport for girls when I was growing up. I was born in 1965 and soccer didn't really take off in the States until the next generation after me. I started to watch a lot of English soccer after I married John in 1991. He was a passionate Liverpool supporter and I fell in love with the game and his team as well.

When I began playing, I had a lot of athletic ability, but not much skill at the game! I learned the tactics really quickly because I watched a lot of soccer on TV but getting my body to do what my mind wanted was really hard and frustrating. I was very athletic and very fast, so I had two things that I could work with which really helped me.

John was born in Liverpool, England, and had played for several years until injury cut short his career. He helped Annette come to grips with the required skills needed to play the game well.

John taught me a lot. I played in San Francisco for about six years, I guess. My first team was very much a social team playing for fun, but as I improved, I moved on to more competitive teams in the Golden Gate Women's League as well as a league in the San Jose area just south of San Francisco.

The couple immigrated to Australia in 1998, and Annette joined South Melbourne when Janette Melvin was there—a highly regarded pioneer of the women's game in Victoria, both as a player and a coach. As a player, Janette represented Victoria in the first national championships in 1975 and was the first woman appointed as a state-level coach. She became a life member of VSF in 2001 and was inducted into the FFV Hall of Fame in 2013. Annette remembers her influence fondly:

When we arrived in Melbourne, the women's leagues were organised very differently to the States. There were fewer teams, the standard was lower overall than in the USA, and the teams were all affiliated with existing men's clubs. Women's soccer has come a long way since then in this country. It has grown tremendously. I joined South Melbourne mainly because I was working in the city and needed to be able to get to training quickly. I considered another team in the city, but South Melbourne seemed more organised and structured. At that time, Janette Melvin was their player/coach, but she was looking for a full-time coach to take over from her.

I really liked Janette and most of the women that I met at South Melbourne. The team had recently been relegated to Division 1 from the Premier League and had lost some of its senior players to other clubs, so they were in a bit of a rebuilding phase. I had become a strong player by then, so was looking forward to being in a competitive, yet friendly environment.

John found himself back coaching as the South Melbourne team lacked one. Although South Melbourne was one of the leading clubs in the league, the women's teams were treated poorly at best.

South Melbourne was the dominant men's team in Australia at the time—winning the 1998 and 1999 grand finals and competing in the 2000 FIFA World Club Championship in Brazil. Although the women's team was allowed to play at the main stadium at Albert Park, once a season, it's probably no surprise that the men who ran the club considered us to be no more important than the junior boys' teams. This is despite the fact that we were playing in the highest women's division, our star player had represented Greece, and we also had an Irish international player for a short time. I don't think our situation was very different to a lot of other women's teams, and it just reflected the fact that most clubs were very much male-dominated places in those days. We played 99% of our home games at Albert Park but had no club rooms and didn't even have the use of those fields for a large part of the year due their closure many weeks prior to the Grand Prix, and several months afterwards while the fields were relaid and repaired. This was an issue for many sports teams who used to have access to Albert Park.

By the end of the 2000 season, South Melbourne was an established Premier League team and had also added a Reserves team. John decided to take a break from coaching at the end of that season and the players found it difficult to recruit a new coach. Annette formed a players committee to organise training venues, registrations and so on, and the committee eventually agreed to take on the boyfriend of one of the players as coach, along with his friend as assistant coach. However, tensions soon developed between him and some of the senior players because of his approach. Issues with how the male coaches treated the women soon arose, which eventually led to the break-up of the team.

> At first, he was really good, but he started doing things like making us carry each other piggyback while we ran and cursing and shouting at everybody

like a drill sergeant. I spoke to him privately at one point to let him know that we didn't respond well to that sort of approach, and it wasn't the way the players wanted to be treated. We had some 14-year-old girls on the team, and the coaching was overly aggressive and disrespectful. I don't think any players respond well to that sort of atmosphere, and it certainly wasn't appropriate for a women's team.

My comments weren't very well received, so after a few more weeks in which things failed to improve, I decided to leave the team. It wasn't an easy decision, because I had invested a lot of time and effort into the club and didn't really want to start over somewhere else. However, I was a 35-year-old professional woman and wasn't prepared to put up with the treatment I was getting. I explained to the other players my reasons for leaving, and although my view was shared by a number of others, the majority of them remained with the club. Fortunately for South Melbourne, the assistant coach took over the team a few months later and he went on to coach them for quite a few seasons.

After the coaching issues, Annette left the club and went to Port Melbourne, which was much more proactive in their treatment of women players.

I went to Port off my own bat because it was the only other city team close to my office. It had just been promoted to the Premier League from the first division, and as a smaller club, was really supportive of its women's team. Their men's team was one of the best in State League, but more than happy to share their ground with us. Unfortunately, they were also without a coach at the time, and were being temporarily coached by the president of the club, Nick Tavanlis, who was a big supporter of women's soccer. After John had seen the facilities and met some of the other supportive committee members there, he allowed himself to be talked into coaching again—at least for a year! It turned out to be three years in the end! Three other players also joined me at Port from South after they saw how supportive the club was, and also, I think, once John started coaching there.

The attitude towards the women's team was much more positive than it had been at South. You could see that in the way the team were treated and in the fact that the club was excited about having a successful women's team. They had people on their committee who did actually care about the women's game and who were trying to do the right thing. We finished a

> creditable fifth in our first season in the Premier League and then pushed Cranbourne all the way in 2002, finishing runners-up that season. In 2002 we had recruited enough players to also field a reserves team in Division 2. There were a number of times that I would play for the Premier team and then for the reserves straight afterward if we were short of players! When I first started playing in the USA, I was a striker because I was quick. Even though I wasn't that skilful, I could run past everybody, and that gave me a 50/50 shot at scoring. (Laughter.) By the time I played at Port I was a sweeper—though I still always fancied getting forward if I could!

During the 1990s, women from different ethnic backgrounds were just starting to become involved in football clubs as players.

> We had very diverse, multinational teams at both South and Port Melbourne. We had lots of different nationalities, in part because those two teams were close to the city and would attract women and girls who either lived, worked or studied in the area. We were fortunate in being able to attract a lot of good players and people. John had a good reputation as a coach and as a creator of a positive environment for female players. As more and more teenage players started entering women's teams from 2000 onwards, parents also wanted the right environment for their daughters, so we were able to create a really positive spirit—especially at Port Melbourne. The women would also try to police each other and have a good sense of camaraderie and let each other know what was okay and what wasn't.

Due to family and work commitments, Annette retired from playing the game in 2005. After hanging up the boots, she remained committed to the development of women's football by taking up a position on the FFV board.

> I stopped playing for Port Melbourne to have a baby. My son was born in 2005, and though I returned for a few games in 2006, I just realised that I didn't have the time or the motivation. You know, partner in a law firm—time was precious and I just couldn't fit everything in—something had to give.

Annette was co-opted onto the FFV board in October 2009. The Annual Report shows Annette as one of only two women directors and states that 'she has been a keen football enthusiast for more than 20 years'. Annette followed in the footsteps of another Victorian women pioneer, as Maggie Koumi had recently resigned from the board in 2007.

> An email had been sent to all the female partners at my firm about an opening on the FV Board. John had been on the FV Women's Committee for a number of years, and I decided it would be good to get involved with the game on a different level. I met with every member of the board in advance, and I was co-opted. Tony Dunkerley, the president of FFV at that time, thought that it was really important to get women representatives on the board and he felt it was a disgrace there wasn't already more female representation at that level.

Annette came to the board just when things were changing for women's football in Victoria. Annette passionately advocated for change. And alongside the FV president, she confronted the ingrained narrowmindedness about women's football and the unchallenged cronyism, which was commonplace within Victorian football.

> Tony had a vision to make football a truly state-wide sport, with an administration which cared as much about the regional areas as the city. He wanted the state teams to be selected on merit rather than coaching politics or whose father knew someone on the selection board. When I was still playing, we once had a young player who would like to have joined our team but was unable to because her state coach wanted her to play for team X, coached by a friend of his. She was told she wouldn't be considered for selection to his state side again if she joined our team! This was reported to the FFV, but nothing was ever done about it. At that time, state team coaches were also allowed to coach club teams, and there was at least one coach we knew who regularly poached state team players for his club side. John used to get very angry about this issue and through the women's league committee tried unsuccessfully to have rules introduced preventing state coaches from being involved in club sides.
>
> I saw a lot of these things change while I was on the Board, and Tony was instrumental in bringing this about.

In 2003 the Crawford Report heralded major changes to the administration and management of football. By 2005, Soccer Australia had become FFA and the women's game had come under its umbrella. And in 2006, a new constitution was developed for the VSF. On its implementation in 2007, the then-FFV board was dissolved, and the board members stood down to make way for the new voting system. The new constitution provided an opportunity for the clubs to be more involved in the running of the federation and provided an avenue for more women to lead.

> One of the most important things was requiring each club to have a constitution. Tony was able to generate a lot of change after the Crawford Report, and I was able to help make those things happen through my support of the plans that Mark Rendell had worked out for the champions league, trying to build up the champions league, trying to get regional sports built up to a level where there were lots of different centres for soccer. Trying to support getting the Knox centre built. Trying to look ahead and also trying to see that the women were supported and had funding. And trying to work, support BSF in working with the Football Federation Australia and working with the professional leagues.

After Tony Dunkerley's time as president ended, Annette, after spending two years as a director, left following internal strife.

> When my two-year term expired, I let it lapse, and Nick Monteleone (chair of FV at the time) made it plain that he did not want me to continue on the Board. I'm not sure I would have continued had he asked me, but I never even had the chance to talk to him about it. Unfortunately, he chose to avoid my calls and emails and wouldn't even do me the courtesy of discussing the matter. Very childish and unprofessional stuff! I did find it hard because I know what proper governance looks like and a lot of those guys didn't seem to know or care about that. They found it difficult to understand the difference between strategy and operations, so you had members of the Board who wanted to run everything in the league, yet not get involved in any overall, long-term strategy to develop the game. That was my great frustration, but I was very proud to have served on the Board with Tony and to support Mark as the CEO and in particular to work with Jamie and Mark Trajcevski who were true professionals.

Although Annette came late to the game in Australia, she is an unsung pioneer of its development and a role model for the many young girls participating in women's football today.

For me, I think I often took a leadership role in the team because I was the oldest woman there. Sometimes, a younger player would discover my age and be freaked out that I was almost the same age as their mother! I hope that changes, and there comes a time when it is common for women of all ages to be involved in clubs as players, coaches and administrators. One of the most rewarding things for me was to be thanked by a parent for being a role model to their teenage daughter, showing them that they could aspire to be a professional woman who played sports and wasn't afraid to be a leader. Those moments made me feel like it was worth putting up with a lot of the other crap we had to deal with.

Look how far we've come

On October 6, 2019, some 40 years later to the day of the Matildas being first officially recognised internationally, the chairman of Football Federation Australia (FFA), Chris Nikou, along with the current Matildas and members of the original team, celebrated the contribution of Australia's first Matildas and the contributions of all involved in the women's game over many years.

'These athletes started a movement, not just a team, which has now become one of the most powerful, popular and recognisable in Australia.'

Later that same year, the Matildas' first official international match was recognised with the placement of a plaque commemorating the game at Seymour Shaw Park, the site of the original match against New Zealand—a first of its kind in this country.

I am excited to see the dedication and hard work of the pioneers of women's football in Australia finally being realised. The generations of women that played the game for the love of it, with no sense of reward, often faced with barriers that many of today's players will never have to face, are now enjoying the recognition and acknowledgement for their efforts. And the sacrifice that many have made in their pursuit to play and stay in the game over the formative years has laid the foundations for the gains that the women's game is now witnessing. The current players are enjoying some of the benefits of the many giant steps taken by women's sport, and football in particular, in recent times.

Times are definitely changing in women's football and as McGowan states, 'we are witnessing some significant lasts and firsts of Australian women's football.' On the back of recent international successes young women now know who the Matildas are and can aspire to be part of one of the leading sporting teams in Australia.

According to a (2019) Benchmark emotional connection study the current Matildas were ranked as Australia's most loved sporting team in 2019. They now have mentors and role models in players such as Sam Kerr to follow and emulate. And they now have a pathway, which is at least partially paid. Improved media attention and the development of social media have lifted the profile of the players and some can now aspire to being household names in Australia.

As a result the sport is now starting to receive the media attention that it deserves, and in amongst the resurging interest in the game, there has emerged a growing desire to recognise the pioneers of the game. There cannot be a clearer example of this transition as that of the current Matildas' captain and leading player Sam Kerr signing a lucrative two-and-a-half-year deal with English club Chelsea FC—reportedly worth $2 million—alongside FFA and Northern NSW Football's recognition of Cheryl Salisbury (1994–2009), former captain of the Matildas being the first Matilda to be inducted into the Sport Australia Hall of Fame.

In 2019 Australia Football Federation Australia (FFA) and the Football Players Association (PFA) announced a landmark collective bargaining agreement (CBA), which sees Matildas receiving the same pay deal as the Socceroos, addressing one of the major issues of gender equity in the game. This agreement came, in no small part, as a result of the players' boycott taken after the conclusion of the 2015 FIFA Women's World Cup in Canada. The strike resulted in the cancellation of the proposed tour to the United States—the first occasion that an Australian team has undertaken such action in the fight for equal rights, and is reminiscent of the battles that the pioneers had to endure to participate in the game. The players were sick and tired of juggling the requirements of elite level football with part-time jobs and in some cases finding new work after having to resign from previous employment in order for them to play. The Agreement also addresses the issues surrounding suitable training facilities, travel and specialist performance support.

The issue of equal pay has been a long-fought battle, and during the Women's World Cup was adopted by the many supporters who backed the players' push for equity—climaxing with the crowd chanting 'equal pay' as the president of FIFA Gianni Infantino awarded the World Cup trophy to the successful US women's national team.

Despite the recent level of success and recognition, there is still a range of major issues which restrict the women's game from reaching its full potential. The chronic under investment by government and football authorities over many years has resulted in a widespread lack of facilities and rising costs associated with registration at the grassroots level. Women and girls have been waiting for 40 years to access improved community facilities—most importantly separate women's change rooms and the availability of suitable playing surfaces. The cost of registration impacts women and girls from minority and migrant communities, and challenges are still presented by an absence of appropriate childcare and suitable medical and psychological support.

The women's semi-professional W-League, which is now 13 years old, is still not a full home and away competition. The game is still only semi-professional with recent reports indicating that almost 50 per cent of W-League players are working at least 21 hours a week outside of football. More recently W-League teams are fighting against the current trend of allocating games on artificial surfaces when A-League teams have access to natural playing surfaces. A recent (2021) W-League report prepared by the PFA has reinforced the calls to address the current structure of the competition, highlighting the need for more matches, a more meaningful and full-time professional calendar, increased remuneration, and raising the minimum workplace standards and facilities for players.

Hosting the 2023 FIFA Women's World Cup will have a lasting impact on the game in Australia and will place the country under the international spotlight. Hopefully, the issues still confronting the women's game will be addressed as part of the build-up to the tournament and have certainly been by Football Australia (FA) in their 'Legacy '23' Plan, which will be presented to government for funding to address some of the historical barriers still facing women in football.

The success of the current Matildas has provided the pioneers with an opportunity to celebrate their achievements. It was great to see a group of players from the 1979 national team on the field at the half-time break of the Chile game in Sydney being applauded by the large crowd. Social media was once more full of congratulations, this time including the rejoicing of past players at functions in the city after the game. Old teammates and friends celebrating both the latest Matildas victory and also the role they played in the development of the game and their place in its long and interesting history.

Moya Dodd, lawyer, former Matilda, prominent women's football advocate, and currently a member of FIFA's Player Status Committee best sums up the contributions of the pioneers of the game and the importance of acknowledging all involved in the journey of women's football in Australia.

> The growth of the Matildas on the world stage certainly helped underscore that we're a serious football country. That growth took millions of actions—all the training sessions, lamington drives, the parents' commitment, the coaches, the canteen helpers, the referees, the players who play a league below the top, holding up the standards and forcing them to improve. The Matildas, and everyone who has built them over 40 years, sit at the top of a pyramid of effort and ambition, where everyone plays their part in lifting them higher.

Acknowledgements

I would like to thank some important people for helping me get this book together. As I mentioned in the Introduction, it is based on my PhD thesis completed in 2016.

First of all I would like to thank my daughter Caitlin who introduced me to the game when she was 11 years of age. Caitlin began her playing career with the Byron Bay Zebras in 1999. She played for several years and was a member of the very successful senior women's team during the early 2000s. I am very happy that she did and I am proud to have shared that journey with her.

I would also like to thank the following people for their contributions, encouragement and advice.

To my wife Gayle, thanks for listening to my constant references to women's football and my many insecurities involved in writing this book. I promise I'll take a break now!

To my family and friends who have remained interested and have supported me throughout the process—thanks. It hasn't been easy and I thank you for your patience and unwavering counsel. Once again I couldn't have done it without your help.

To my friends in football: Ian Syson, Paul Mavroudis, Roy Hay and Maggie Koumi, Lee McGowan and Fiona Crawford, Ted Simmons, Heather Reid AM, Jean Williams, Trixie Tagg, Lyn Wright (nee McKernan), Greg Werner, Samantha Lewis and Peter Eedy. Thank you for the advice and help along the way.

A special thank you to Bonita Mersiades of Fair Play Publishing for giving me this opportunity. My heartfelt thanks.

And an enormous thank you to all the women (and men) who kindly shared their time and stories with me. It has been a pleasure to meet you.

About the Author

Dr Greg Downes is a sessional academic and completed his PhD thesis in 2016 with Victoria University, in Melbourne, Australia. The thesis is titled: *An oral history of women's football in Australia,* and looks at what the oral testimony of women who were pioneers of the game of football contribute to the understandings of gender and football history in Australia. The research is based on interviews with women (and men), some of whom have represented Australia, other players, administrators and referees.

Greg became interested in researching women's football due to the involvement of his youngest daughter Caitlin. While studying for his Master's, he used examples of the injustices and discrimination faced by women involved in football as topics for his research, and came to realise that little or no research had been done on the history of women's football in Australia.

Greg completed his master's degree research project in 2008 titled *Returning to its Roots: The Future of Women's Football in the Asian Football Confederation (AFC),* and has since collaborated on a number of academic articles on the history of women's football with Ian Syson, Roy Hay and Lee McGowan.

Greg currently writes, teaches and researches in women's sport history, sport management and human services at Southern Cross University in Lismore, where he is a sessional unit assessor in sport management in the School of Health and Human Services. He has a bachelor's degree in economics and a master's degree in international sport management.

Note from the Publisher

As noted by Greg Downes, this book is based on some of the pioneers who formed the basis of his PhD thesis and represent only a drop in the ocean of the stories and information held by those who were part of the history of women's football in Australia.

There is significant scope for more research, more stories and more history.

At Fair Play Publishing, we are on a mission to share Australia's football history and culture through books. As a niche publishing house founded by a woman who has been involved in football for a lifetime, we would be delighted to publish more stories not only about the women's game, but also about women in the game.

When we first formed, we approached several writers specifically about writing something about women players or other women involved in the game. None have been forthcoming; although I am pleased that, in addition to the *Encyclopedia of Matildas* published first in 2019 and updated in 2020, many of our books have at least incorporated aspects of the history of the women's game. Another book, *The World Cup Chronicles — 31 Days that Rocked Brazil*, had a woman on the front cover and included a chapter entitled *Marta is better than Pelé*. We even published a novel with a female footballer as the main character, *Anna Black*, under our Popcorn Press imprint.

I believe there are plenty of ideas that arise from this book. We hope it gives aspiring authors inspiration to follow in Greg's footsteps and find and write the stories of women's football and women in football. I know that we would be more than happy to publish them.

Bonita Mersiades
Publisher

More books from Fair Play Publishing

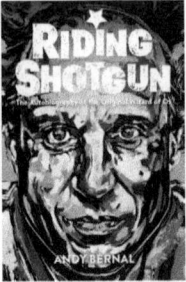

Encyclopedia of Matildas
Andrew Howe and Greg Werner

Riding Shotgun — the Autobiography of the Original Wizard of Oz
by Andy Bernal

Be My Guest — Football Superstars in Australia
Jason Goldsmith and Lucas Gillard

Code Wars — The Battle for Fans, Dollars and Survival
Dr Hunter Fujak

Coming Soon

Portraits in Football
Bonita Mersiades

100 Years of Football at Wynnum
Vicky Krayem

The Itinerant Coach – The Life and Footballing Times of Steve Darby
Antony Sutton

Books from Popcorn Press
(an imprint of Fair Play Publishing)

Anna Black — this girl can play
Texi Smith

Jarrod Black Guilty Party
Texi Smith

www.ingramcontent.com/pod-product-compliance
Lightning Source LLC
Chambersburg PA
CBHW071733080526
44588CB00013B/2005